DiMaggio jumped on Hatten's first pitch and slashed a bullet in the direction of the low bullpen fence in left. The Yankees in the dugout stood up to watch the flight of the ball. A roar escaped from the crowd.

"Swung on, belted, it's a long one," shouted radio play-by-play announcer Red Barber. "Deep into left center . . ."

Little five-foot-six-inch Al Gionfriddo, who had just come into the game, began sprinting toward the bullpen. Gionfriddo had hit a meager .177 for the Dodgers during the season, and his career in baseball was shaky. He worked as a fireman during the off-season.

They didn't have cushy padded outfield walls in 1947. There were concrete walls and sharp fences. The ball was starting its descent and Gionfriddo could tell it was going to land near the low wire fence. A sign on the wall indicated it was 415 feet from home plate.

"Back goes Gionfriddo!" yelled Red Barber. "Back, back, back, back, back . . ."

WORLD SERIES
SERIES
Classics

♦ ♦ ♦ ♦ ♦ ♦ ♦ ♦

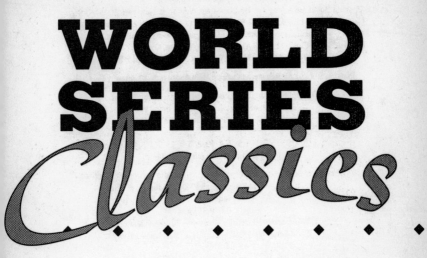

WORLD SERIES Classics

• • • • • •

DAN GUTMAN

PUFFIN BOOKS

PUFFIN BOOKS

Published by the Penguin Group

Penguin Books USA Inc., 375 Hudson Street, New York, New York 10014, U.S.A.
Penguin Books Ltd, 27 Wrights Lane, London W8 5TZ, England
Penguin Books Australia Ltd, Ringwood, Victoria, Australia
Penguin Books Canada Ltd, 10 Alcorn Avenue, Toronto, Ontario, Canada M4V 3B2
Penguin Books (N.Z.) Ltd, 182-190 Wairau Road, Auckland 10, New Zealand

Penguin Books Ltd, Registered Offices: Harmondsworth, Middlesex, England

First published in the United States of America by Viking,
a division of Penguin Books USA Inc., 1994
Published in Puffin Books, 1996

1 3 5 7 9 10 8 6 4 2

Copyright © Dan Gutman, 1994

THE LIBRARY OF CONGRESS HAS CATALOGED THE VIKING EDITION AS FOLLOWS:
Gutman, Dan. World Series classics / Dan Gutman. p. cm.
Includes index
ISBN 0-670-85286-4
1. World Series (Baseball)—History—Juvenile literature.
[1. World Series (Baseball)—History. 2. Baseball—History.]
I. Title.
GV878.4.G89 1994 796.357'646—dc20 94–11591 CIP AC

Printed in the United States of America

Puffin Books ISBN 0-14-037751-4

Acknowledgments

Thanks to Elizabeth Law, Nina Putignano, Phil Airoldi, and Tom Lynch at Viking, Liza Voges and Julie Alperen at Kirchoff/Wohlberg, Pat Kelly at the National Baseball Hall of Fame, Nat Andriani at the Associated Press, David Pietrusza at the Society for American Baseball Research, David Kelly at the Library of Congress, George Brace, Mike Lattman, and, of course, Nina.

To kids who hate to read
but love baseball

Contents

FOR ANY BASEBALL FAN, October is the most exciting time of year because that's when the World Series takes place. During the Series, every play is magnified. There are no second chances. The pressure is on. Sixty million people or more are watching on TV.

Anything can happen. Maybe Carlton Fisk will stroke an extra-inning, game-winning homer that will be remembered for decades. Or maybe a pebble near third base will cause a bad hop over the head of Fred Lindstrom and cost his team the championship.

Since the modern World Series began in 1903, some of the showdowns have been boring, but many have been exciting, hard-fought contests. *Five* of them have been truly *spectacular*, with stomach-churning intensity and riveting, gripping action. Melodrama and strategy. Heroes and goats. Seesaw battles to the end.

In this book you'll experience the play-by-play of the *best* World Series in the history of baseball—1991, 1975, 1947, 1924 and 1912. These World Series had a kind of motionless tension that makes true fans shake their heads when people who don't like the game say baseball is dull. I've made every effort to describe these games for you as if you were sitting in the best seat of the ballpark.

Game 1 of the 1912 World Series is about to begin. So take your seat, grab a hot dog, and enjoy the most exciting baseball that has ever been played.

—Dan Gutman

The Stars of This Book

(in order of appearance)

1912
John McGraw
Fred Snodgrass
Christy Mathewson
Rube Marquard
Tris Speaker
Smokey Joe Wood
Duffy Lewis
Harry Hooper

1924
Walter Johnson
Fred Lindstrom
Frank Frisch
Bill Terry
Sam Rice
Bucky Harris
Goose Goslin
Roger Peckinpaugh

1947
Jackie Robinson
Eddie Stanky
Pee Wee Reese
Carl Furrillo
Hugh Casey
Joe DiMaggio

Phil Rizzuto
Tommy Henrich
Yogi Berra
Joe Page

1975
Tony Perez
Johnny Bench
Pete Rose
Joe Morgan
Ken Griffey
Carl Yastrzemski
Fred Lynn
Dwight Evans
Carlton Fisk
Luis Tiant

1991
Steve Avery
John Smoltz
Tom Glavine
David Justice
Terry Pendleton
Mark Lemke
Lonnie Smith
Kirby Puckett
Jack Morris

CHAPTER

1

1912

New York Giants

vs.

Boston Red Sox

The First Great World Series

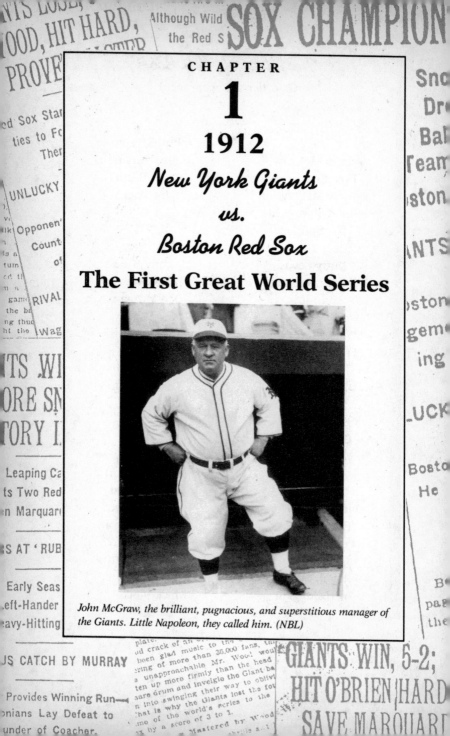

John McGraw, the brilliant, pugnacious, and superstitious manager of the Giants. Little Napoleon, they called him. (NBL)

Idol of Boston
Red Sox into
ball pennant,
looked to brir

BEDIENT IS STAR
OF WORLD SERIE
LD SERIE

ss
asy
ting
es $'
ning

er Opposes Ve
son and Holds
o Three Hits.

PLO

HES OLD FOF

'An;
Star
vd D

Weakness in t
No Red Sox
First Base.

H S

N WINNING R

gues
res

rly Favors t
g and Speake
heir Quarrel.

IN THE FIEL

al to
N, M:
worl
e of
ck.
rath
hurr

arade After V
ent Escapes a
Clubhouse.

BOSTON W.
WOODSTOF
IN NINTH I

x Pitcher Pales
ants Hit Safely, b
e with Strikeouts

Giants centerfielder Fred Snodgrass made perhaps the most famous error in baseball history. But it was two walks and a dropped pop-up in the same inning that really decided the 1912 World Series. (NBL)

League championsm,,

such a hurry that he gave away

championship. It was because

muff of an easy

es a Fly, Giv
and Then Boston
les on the Ozark Giant.

McGRAW BLAMES MEYER

His Signal B
to Yerr

SETS TESREAU

Sno

PL

*I*T WAS MONDAY NIGHT, the night before the World Series, and the streets of Manhattan were jumping. Three hundred crazed Red Sox fans who called themselves the Royal Rooters were marching and dancing down Broadway. Leading the parade in his silk hat was the flamboyant mayor of Boston, John "Honey Fitz" Fitzgerald. His grandson—John F. Kennedy—would one day be president of the United States.

Directly behind Honey Fitz marched a 30-piece brass band, booming Boston's lucky song, "Tessie." The Royal Rooters carried their trusty songbooks (*Battle Songs of the Red Sox*) as well as red flags, horns, megaphones, and torches that lit up the night. On their hatbands were the words, *Oh, You Red Sox!* Around their waists they wore sashes made of—what else?—red socks.

New Yorkers lining the streets hissed and booed. They, of course, hated the Red Sox. The rivalry between New York and Boston has been going on for some time.

The New York Giants had cruised to the National League championship by ten games, their second pennant in a row. The surprising Red Sox, who had finished fifth the year before, won 105 games to overwhelm the rest of the American League by 14 games. Now these two teams were to meet in the ninth modern World Series to determine which one could call itself the best team in baseball.

For three nights, fans had been waking up the night watchman at the Polo Grounds in hopes that he had tickets to sell. When the ticket office finally opened its windows at nine o'clock on Monday morning, thousands of people were waiting. Bleacher seats were just $1, but fans were offering as much as $200 for them. Some people made money by selling their place in line.

People were desperate to get inside the Polo Grounds. They wouldn't be able to listen to the World Series on the radio. There *was* no radio in 1912.

THE PLAYERS. The New York Giants could play brilliantly at times, but sometimes looked like a bunch of minor leaguers. With strong pitching and baserunning, they almost always won. But when their defense fell apart, they could be beaten by just about anybody.

The Giants were led by the legendary John McGraw, their hard-driving, pugnacious manager. In the infield was Buck Herzog (.263 for the season) at third, Art Fletcher (.282) at short, Captain Larry "Laughing" Doyle (.330) at second, and Fred Merkle (.309) at first. The outfield was patrolled by Josh Devore (.275) in left, Fred Snodgrass (.269) in center, and Red Murray (.277) in right. Chief Jack Meyers was behind the plate. Meyers was a Mission Indian who had hit a stinging .358 for the season.

SNODGRASS, N. Y., NAT'L   MERKLE, N. Y. NAT'L   DEVORE, NEW YORK NAT'L

The Giant pitching ace was "Big Six"—13-year veteran Christy Mathewson. Matty no longer had his overpowering fastball, but he still won 23 games with his "faders," his "floaters," and his intelligence. Rumors were going around that Mathewson had added a secret weapon to his arsenal—a spitball—and that he was going to spring it on the Red Sox. The spitter was a legal pitch in 1912.

The Giants also had left-hander Rube Marquard, who had a remarkable season. Rube, who was Mathewson's roommate on road trips, won his first start of the season and just kept going. He won 19 games in a row and 26 by the end of the year.

MATHEWSON, N. Y. NAT'L.   MEYERS, N. Y. NAT'L.   MURRAY, N. Y. NAT'L.

On Thursday before the World Series, Mathewson and Marquard made a secret trip to Boston to watch the Red Sox play and spot their weaknesses.

They didn't find many. In centerfield was Tris Speaker, a former Texas rodeo rider and telegraph lineman whom the Red Sox had picked up for $500. Spoke had had a spectacular year, hitting .383. He stole 53 bases and led the American League in doubles. With Speaker flanked by George "Duffy" Lewis (.284) in left and Harry Hooper (.242) in right, Boston had one of the best fielding outfields of all time.

The infield was tight, too, with Larry Gardner (.315) at third, Heinie Wagner (.274) at short, Steve Yerkes (.252) at second, and player/manager Jake Stahl (.301) at first. Stahl was a big, easygoing man who had retired from baseball the previous year to become a banker. When the owners of the Red Sox offered him the manager's job, he decided to come back.

One overpowering pitcher can dominate a short series, and the Red Sox had just the guy who could do it in Smokey Joe Wood. Just 22 years old, Wood was one of the fastest in the game. He threw the ball so hard, he worried about killing somebody if a fastball got away from him. Wood got his nickname after a teammate exclaimed, "He sure can smoke 'em!"

During the regular season, Smokey Joe won an astonishing 34 games against just 5 losses. Ten of the victories were shutouts. His ERA was 1.91. If you know baseball, you know those are Hall of Fame numbers. To make things even tougher on his opponents, Wood would let loose a spitball now and then.

Wood's only problem was that he was so nervous going into the World Series that he couldn't speak. His roommate, Tris Speaker, did the best he could to calm the young star down.

CARRIGAN, BOSTON AMER.   WAGNER, BOSTON AMER.   SPEAKER, BOSTON AMER.

Catching duties for Boston were shared by Hick Cady (.259) and Bill "Rough" Carrigan (.263).

Going into Game 1, the Red Sox were favorites, but not by much. *New York Times* baseball analyst Hugh Fullerton wrote, "It will be a hard fought series and the winner will have to battle to the bitter end for a victory."

He didn't know how right he would be.

GAME 1. Tuesday, October 8. There were 35,730 fans crammed into New York's Polo Grounds. Three thousand more were gathered on a hill outside, a vantage point from which they could only see the leftfielder's *legs*. Still, they were happy. The color of the leftfielder's socks indicated which team was in the field, and the roar of the crowd provided clues about what was going on.

Thousands of other baseball fans jamming Times Square several miles away actually had a better view of the World Series. The games were "recreated" on a giant electrical board outside the offices of *The New York Times*. Every pitch was transmitted instantaneously from the ballpark by telegraph.

There was no radio or TV in 1912, so fans who couldn't get tickets to the game jammed Times Square to watch a telegraphed re-creation of the World Series on this board outside the New York Times offices.

At the Polo Grounds, a billboard passed this important information to the fans: *Be Cool. Wear Loose-Fitting Underwear.*

A roar came from the crowd as the Giants took the field, warming up in their new violet-trimmed uniforms and maroon sweaters. (The windbreaker didn't exist in 1912). As expected, Christy Mathewson was loosening up. But throwing alongside him was 22-year-old rookie spitballer Jeff Tesreau. Ozark Jeff was 17–7 for the season, with a no-hitter to his credit and a league-leading 1.96 earned run average. Giants manager John McGraw had both pitchers warming up because he didn't want to let the Red Sox know who his starter would be until the last minute.

Before the serious business of playing baseball could begin, various ceremonies had to be completed. Giants second baseman Larry Doyle received a car for winning the Chalmers Award, which was what the Most Valuable Player Award was called in those days. The Royal Rooters belted out a few stanzas of "Tessie" for good luck, with Honey Fitz singing loudest of all. Baseball celebrities such as Walter Johnson, Ty Cobb, and Cy Young were escorted to their seats. New York Mayor Gaynor threw out the first ball. Photographers snapped pictures of everything.

Finally, the fans settled into their seats and at precisely 2:07 PM, umpire Bill Klem shouted the two words baseball fans love to hear—"Play ball!"

Out of the Giants dugout stepped . . . Jeff Tesreau.

"What's the matter with Matty?" shouted concerned Giants fans.

As John McGraw explained later, he picked the rookie Tesreau to start because he believed Tesreau's spitball would fool the Red Sox. McGraw was saving Mathewson, a veteran, for Game 2 on enemy turf in Boston. The press had another view of the decision—McGraw was afraid of Smokey Joe Wood. Wood was so strong, McGraw didn't want to waste his best man against him.

Tesreau looked in for the sign, wet the ball and threw the first pitch of the 1912 World Series to Harry Hooper. Ball one. The next three were out of the strike zone too, and Hooper strolled to first.

Tesreau looked shaky, but he settled down and retired the next three Sox.

In the bottom of the first, Joe Wood blew away the first Giants hitter with a strikeout. Both pitchers kept the scoreboard blank through the first two innings.

Leading off the third for the Giants, Tesreau struck out. But Josh Devore walked, and, with Larry Doyle coming up, John McGraw decided to put on the hit-and-run play—the runner takes off with the pitch and the batter tries to slap the ball through the hole vacated by the infielder covering second.

Doyle hit a blooper near the leftfield line. Boston leftfielder Duffy Lewis hesitated, peering into the sun, and the ball dropped in front of him. With runners at second and third, Wood struck out Fred Snodgrass on three pitches for the second out.

Red Murray was up. In the 1911 World Series, Murray had had *no* hits in 21 at-bats, and Giants fans had been so angry that they'd hung a dummy labeled Red Murray from a lamppost near the Polo Grounds. Murray remembered. This time he slammed a single up the middle to drive in Devore and Doyle.

Murray was thrown out trying to stretch his single into a double, but the Giants had the lead, 2–0.

That was how it remained until the sixth inning. Jeff Tesreau was working on a no-hitter and Giants manager McGraw was looking like a genius for letting him start the Series instead of Mathewson. But then Tesreau's luck ran out.

Tris Speaker limbered up by swinging three bats, and then tossing two of them aside. With one out in the sixth, Speaker rapped a line drive to left centerfield, between Devore and Snodgrass. The two outfielders converged on the ball. It was Devore's play, but he gave way to Snodgrass.

Snow, as he was called, misjudged the ball. It ticked off his glove. As Speaker tore around the bases, the ball rolled to the fence. He held up with a triple. When Duffy Lewis grounded to second, Speaker came home to make the score Giants 2, Sox 1.

In centerfield, Fred Snodgrass hung his head. But this would not be his biggest mistake of the World Series.

In the next inning, Tesreau fell apart. With one out, Boston shortstop Heinie Wagner singled hard to center. Hick Cady, the catcher, followed with a bloop single, putting runners at first and third. Smokey Joe Wood hit a grounder to second. It should have been a double play to retire the side, but Larry Doyle fell as he was fielding the ball and could only get the force play at second. Two outs.

Heinie Wagner had foolishly held at third on the force play, but Harry Hooper slashed a double down the first-base line and Wagner trotted home. Giants 2, Sox 2.

Tesreau got two strikes on Steve Yerkes, but the Boston second baseman then ripped a scorching single to left on a pitch near his eyes. Wood and Hooper dashed home and suddenly it was Sox 4, Giants 2. The Royal Rooters erupted, dancing the turkey trot to the tune of "The Marseillaise."

The Giants were still down by two runs as they came up for their last licks in the bottom of the ninth. With one out, Fred Merkle attacked the first pitch and sent a single just beyond Wagner's reach into leftfield. Buck Herzog followed with another single. The tying run was on base and Chief Meyers strode to the plate. Wood appeared to be tiring. Meyers took a cut at the first pitch and slammed a double off the wall, scoring Fred Merkle. Three hits in a row for the Giants. Sox 4, Giants 3.

Runners on second and third. One out. A long fly ball would tie the game, a hit could win it. Giants fans were screaming. *The New York Times* wrote of Joe Wood, "His face paled and his jaws were set tightly as he faced the frenzied multitude, which howled for his downfall."

Manager Jake Stahl trotted over to the mound. "Keep cool, Joe, old boy. You can get this fellow." Stahl instructed Wood to throw nothing but fastballs. He needed strikeouts to prevent those runners from scoring.

Wood bore down and fanned Art Fletcher for the second out. It was his tenth strikeout of the game.

The last hope for the Giants was their best pinch hitter, Doc Crandall, who hit .313 for the year. Wood worked Crandall to a full count. He had thrown 121 pitches by that time and didn't have many left.

Wood threw his next fastball waist high on the inside corner. Crandall took a futile cut at it and missed. Game 1 was over. Sox 4, Giants 3. Jake Stahl ran to the mound and hugged Joe Wood.

After the game, Wood described the last strikeout for reporters—"I threw so hard I thought my arm would fly right off my body."

Game 2 would be in Boston the next day. The Wright Brothers had flown only nine years earlier, so taking a plane between cities was out of the question. A train was held at Grand Central Station, and the players rushed to get on it. They would have five hours to think about Game 1 and prepare for the next one.

GAME 2. Fenway Park, which is one of the oldest ballparks today, was brand-spanking-new in 1912. The leftfield wall, which everyone calls the Green Monster, was just a low wall with advertisements plastered over it in those days. There was a steep hill leading up to the wall. Many outfielders tripped and fell while chasing long drives, but Boston leftfielder Duffy Lewis was so smooth out there that the hill became known as Duffy's Cliff.

There was a sprinkling of rain in the morning, but the sun broke through, and Bostonians came out in force to cheer their heroes. The Royal Rooters were even more boisterous on their home turf. Their brass band taunted the Giants, playing "We'll Do the Same Thing Over Again." Mayor Honey Fitz presented a big red car to Jake Stahl and a solid silver bat to Heinie Wagner.

Christy Mathewson was on the mound for the Giants, but he got into deep trouble right off the bat. Three infield hits filled the bases. A double down the third-base line by Jake Stahl netted three runs for Boston. There was no sign of Matty's rumored spitball.

A lesser pitcher than Mathewson would have been replaced. But manager McGraw stuck with his ace, and Matty settled down.

Meanwhile, his teammates fought back with their bats, picking up a run in the second and another one in the fourth off left-hander Ray Collins. The Sox scored again in the fifth, making it a 4–2 ballgame going into the eighth inning. If the Giants lost Game 2, it would be nearly impossible to come back and win the World Series.

But Fred Snodgrass started the eighth with a low liner

to left that bounced off Duffy Lewis's hands. Then Larry Doyle hit a bullet up the middle. Runners on first and second. Beals Becker, playing in place of Josh Devore for the day, hit into a force play. Snodgrass advanced to third. He scored on a long double to left by the hot-hitting Red Murray. Sox 4, Giants 3.

That was the end of Ray Collins. Charley Hall came in to replace him for Boston, and Hall got Fred Merkle to foul out. That brought up Buck Herzog. With a 2–2 count, he popped up behind the plate. Catcher Bill Carrigan circled under it but the wind blew the ball back toward the plate. As Carrigan caught it off balance, the ball fell out of his mitt. Herzog's at-bat was spared, and he said his thank-you by whaling a double to right. Two more runs scored, and it was Giants 5, Sox 4.

The Red Sox weren't quitters. In the bottom of the eighth, Duffy Lewis doubled to left with two outs. Red Murray crashed into the wall chasing the ball. As Murray was lying on the grass catching his breath, a fan grabbed his cap. Another one was sent out from the Giants bench.

Next up, Larry Gardner hit a shot through Art Fletcher's legs at short. Duffy Lewis raced home, and the game was tied at 5–5. Boston might have scored more, but Mathewson fanned Heinie Wagner to end the inning. Neither team scored in the ninth, so extra innings were in order.

Fred Merkle started the tenth with a tremendous drive, a triple off the leftfield fence. Moose McCormick, baseball's best pinch hitter, hit a sacrifice fly to score Merkle. The Giants would have liked to score an "insurance run," but were happy to go into the bottom of the tenth leading 6–5.

"The last half of the tenth is as sad, neighbor, as a jumping toothache," commented *The New York Times*.

It was only sad from the New York point of view. What happened was that Tris Speaker slammed a drive to the centerfield wall. By the time the Giants relayed the ball to the infield, Speaker was rounding third.

Buck Herzog threw a hip at him as Speaker touched the bag. It slowed Speaker down, but he didn't fall and he didn't stop, either. He was going for an inside-the-park homer to tie the game.

Reserve catcher Art Wilson braced himself at home. Play at the plate. The ball was there ahead of the runner. But Speaker slid in hard, and the ball popped out of Wilson's grasp. Umpire Silk O'Loughlin threw out his hands and shouted, "Safe!" so every fan in Fenway Park could hear. Speaker reached back and hugged the plate just to be on the safe side.

Red Sox fans erupted with joy. Sox 6. Giants 6.

Tris Speaker, who was angry about Herzog's football block, got up and charged toward Buck Herzog at third. Both benches emptied as the two men fought until the umpires broke it up.

Nobody scored in the eleventh inning. Mathewson, still going strong, retired the side with just three pitches. He hadn't walked a batter all afternoon.

The sky had grown dark by the end of the inning, and there were no stadium lights or night games in those days. After a short consultation with the other umpires, Silk O'Loughlin raised his right arm and yelled, "Game called on account of darkness!"

The long hits, the great plays, Matty's pitching effort— all wasted. The tired warriors would do it all over again the next day in Boston.

GAME 3. Before game time, Tris Speaker was given a new car for winning the American League Chalmers Award. Speaker took a few wild laps around the ballpark in it, amusing and terrifying the crowd. He also shook hands with Buck Herzog, and the two apologized to each other for their brawl the day before.

Then it came time for the serious business of the championship of the world. Boston sent Buck O'Brien to the mound, a spitballer who had a 20–13 record for the season. For the Giants it was Rube Marquard. After his 19-game winning streak, Marquard faltered in the second half of the season, winning just 7 games while losing 11. There was some concern that he'd blown out his arm.

But Marquard had the Red Sox hitters at his mercy, tossing a five-hit shutout through eight innings. Not one Boston baserunner reached third, and only two reached second.

O'Brien pitched a good game, too. The Giants only got

seven hits, but they put a few together at the right time to scratch out a run in the second inning and another in the fifth. Red Murray helped protect that lead with a diving, twisting leap into the stands to catch what would have been a home run for Heinie Wagner. Going into the bottom of the ninth, the score was Giants 2, Sox 0.

It was past five o'clock by that time, and a fog had drifted into Fenway Park from Massachusetts Bay. It created an eerie scene—rightfield had just about disappeared into the mist.

Tris Speaker led off by popping out to short. Duffy Lewis bounced to Fred Merkle at first. That should have been the second out of the inning, but Marquard didn't get off the mound quickly enough to cover first, and Lewis beat it out. Next, Larry Gardner slammed a double into the rightfield corner. As the ball bounced around out there, Duffy Lewis came all the way around to score. Giants 2, Sox 1.

Boston fans had been waiting for something to cheer about all afternoon, and the stands were rocking. Marquard had thrown 120 pitches by that time, and he was looking wobbly.

Larry Gardner was on second with one out. Jake Stahl was up, and he hit a high bouncer up the middle. Gardner thought the ball was going to go through the infield, so he set off for third base. But Marquard leaped up, speared the ball, and threw it to third to get Gardner for second out. Stahl made it to first safely.

Next, Heinie Wagner slapped a grounder to short. Art Fletcher picked the ball cleanly, but Fred Merkle dropped the throw at first base. Stahl daringly went all the way to third. Once again the Giants defense was collapsing.

Boston had the tying run at third, the winning run at first. Two outs. The crowd was on its feet now, screaming for a Boston hit.

The batter was Hick Cady, the catcher. On the first pitch, Heinie Wagner stole second. Runners on second and third. Now the winning run could score on a single. It was getting dark, and everyone knew this could be the last inning.

Marquard threw and Cady swung. It was a long drive to the gap in right center. The Boston runners took off from second and third. Deep in the rightfield fog, Josh Devore took off with the crack of the bat. Running to his left and away from the plate, he leaped at the last possible instant with both hands in the air.

Most of the crowd couldn't see what happened next. They just saw the two runners cross the plate. If Devore caught the ball, the Giants had won. If the ball had gotten past Devore, the Sox were winners in a terrific come-from-behind victory. Boston fans let out a roar, preferring to believe Devore couldn't have possibly made the catch.

But he *did*. The little five-foot-six-inch speedster snared the ball on a dead run. He never stopped running, dashing right into the Giants clubhouse in centerfield. Some said it was the greatest catch ever. We'll never know, as this was the pre-video age.

That night sportswriter Fred Lieb was in his Boston hotel when he heard a fan say, "Boston wins! What a great game for the Sox to pull out!"

"But the Sox lost," Lieb corrected him. "The Giants won, 2–1."

"What do you mean!" the fan replied angrily. "I was there, and the Red Sox beat Marquard in the ninth, 3–2. I should take a punch at your nose!"

Lieb took the man over to the newsstand, where the evening papers were being piled. The headline in *The Boston American* read: GIANTS WIN THIRD GAME; TIE SERIES.

Lieb didn't get punched in the nose. The word spread across Boston that the Sox had lost the game. It was back to New York for Game 4.

GAME 4.   It had rained all night and the Polo Grounds was muddy. It looked like the game might be called off, but at noon the umpires gave the go-ahead to play. The Royal Rooters stayed home in Boston, but three Red Sox fans showed up at the ballpark with baseballs—each fan claiming *his* ball had gotten past Josh Devore to end the previous game.

It was Smokey Joe Wood against Jeff Tesreau again, both pitchers working on just two days of rest. This game wasn't as tense as the last three. Wood held New York scoreless through six innings. Heinie Wagner saved him with three sparkling fielding plays at shortstop that reminded fans of the great Honus Wagner of the Pittsburgh Pirates.

Tesreau pitched better than he had in Game 1. He was nicked for a run in the second when Larry Gardner tripled to rightfield and came home on a wild pitch. Boston pushed across another run in the fourth on a walk, fielder's choice, stolen base, and a single. Sox 2, Giants 0.

The Giants had their best chance in the seventh. Smokey Joe struck out Fred Merkle, but Buck Herzog singled sharply in the hole between third and short. Chief Meyers flied out to center for the second out.

Wood didn't worry about the next hitter, Art Fletcher, very much. Fletcher had just one hit in 14 at-bats. But this time he crashed a ball off the rightfield wall for a double. Herzog scored from first, and it was Sox 2, Giants 1.

Moose McCormick was sent up to pinch hit for Jeff Tesreau. On second was Art Fletcher, representing the tying run. McCormick whacked a shot off the legs of second baseman Steve Yerkes. As the ball rolled, Fletcher rounded third. Manager John McGraw, who sometimes coached third, took a big chance and gave Fletcher the green light to try and score. He wanted that tying run badly.

Yerkes picked up the rolling ball and whipped it to the

plate. It was there well ahead of Fletcher. He knew he would have to jar the ball loose from Hick Cady to score. Fletcher came in hard, crashing into Cady and flying headfirst a few feet over him. But in the end, Cady still had the ball in his hand for the third out of the inning. The score remained Sox 2, Giants 1.

Nobody scored in the eighth, and Boston picked up another run in the top of the ninth with an RBI single from Smokey Joe Wood. Sox 3, Giants 1. In Times Square, dejected Giants fans began walking away from the big electric scoreboard.

"Stick to the end," bellowed one diehard rooter. "It's not over until the last ball is pitched."

But minutes later the last ball *was* pitched, and Boston had defeated the Giants to take a 2–1 lead in games. As Joe Wood walked off the mound, a woman sitting near the Boston dugout tossed him a bouquet of flowers.

Before the Giants boarded the train to Boston, John McGraw invoked the words of naval hero John Paul Jones—"We have just begun to fight!"

GAME 5. Saturday, Columbus Day. It was another dark and misty morning, but Fenway Park was sold out by noon. The president of the United States, William Taft, had requested that updates of the game be sent to him by wireless on his yacht near Newport, Rhode Island.

During practice, some Red Sox fans ran on the field and grabbed a few baseballs for souvenirs. Fred Snodgrass threw a ball at them. The Fenway fans booed, and they would hoot at the Giants centerfielder for the entire game.

Christy Mathewson was on the mound for the Giants again, this time facing a raw rookie named Hugh Bedient. Bedient was 11 years old when Matty broke into the majors, and he grew up worshiping the Giants star. Now he was to pitch against his idol in the World Series.

Bedient (20–9 during the season) showed his nervousness, walking Josh Devore on four pitches to start the game. But then he settled down and retired the side. Mathewson had pitched 11 fruitless innings in Game 2 and had every right to be tired. He gave up a single to Harry Hooper on his first pitch of the game. But he too settled down. The game was scoreless after two innings.

Harry Hooper was up again in the third, and he walloped Matty's slow ball deep to left for a triple. On the next pitch, Steve Yerkes slammed a drive just as hard to center. It sailed over Fred Snodgrass and bounced off the wall at a crazy angle. When all was said and done, Yerkes was parked at third and Hooper in the dugout with the first run of the game. Sox 1, Giants 0.

Tris Speaker liked Mathewson's first pitch, too, and he ripped a hot grounder toward second. Larry Doyle couldn't make the play, and Yerkes came home from third. The other Red Sox were unable to pile on more runs, but Boston led 2–0.

After that, Mathewson's jaw was clenched. He didn't

Tris Speaker was the heart, soul, and centerfielder of the Red Sox. His .344 lifetime average is seventh highest in baseball history, and he ranks first in doubles, fifth in hits, sixth in triples, and eighth in runs. (NBL)

allow another baserunner for the rest of the game, retiring 17 Red Sox in a row.

But it wasn't enough. On the day "Columbus discovered America," America discovered Hugh Bedient. The hero of Boston went all the way, giving up just three hits, one of them a single by his hero Christy Mathewson. Bedient didn't have much of a curveball, but his high fastballs corralled the Giants. They could only manage one run in the seventh, and that came on an error. Final score: Sox 2, Giants 1.

Boston fans rushed the field, singing, shouting, clanging cowbells and anything else that could make noise. They tried to hoist Bedient up on their shoulders, but the young pitcher rushed to the happy Boston clubhouse.

Exhausted, Christy Mathewson walked to the Giants bench with his head bowed. He put on his mackinaw coat and disappeared into the clubhouse. In two games he had pitched 19 solid innings, and all he had to show for his efforts was a loss and a tie. Giants fans remembered the days when *nobody* could beat the great Mathewson. Afterwards, Matty told reporters he'd thrown his arm out, and that his career was probably finished.

Boston led the World Series three games to one. Six months earlier, the Titanic had sunk off the coast of Newfoundland on its maiden voyage. The New York Giants looked like they'd also hit an iceberg and were going down. The table was set for Smokey Joe Wood to wrap up the series on Monday.

"We are not beaten yet," said the always-battling John McGraw. "We are going to fight every step of the way, and I am sure of one thing, which is that once we catch the Red Sox we will beat them in the deciding game."

GAME 6. On the train to New York, Red Sox owner Jim McAleer decided he wanted Buck O'Brien—the loser of Game 3—to pitch Game 6 instead of Smokey Joe Wood. McAleer told manager Jake Stahl that pitching O'Brien would give Wood an extra day of rest, and Wood could come back and pitch Game 7 if Boston lost Game 6. Stahl protested, but McAleer called the shots.

It was a bad decision. O'Brien didn't have it that day. The Giants jumped all over him in the first inning. With one out, Larry Doyle beat out a grounder to second and promptly stole second. Snodgrass whiffed, but Murray beat out a grounder to short, advancing Doyle to third. Fred Merkle was up when O'Brien suddenly whirled toward first base and faked a throw. Umpire Bill Klem called a balk. That sent Doyle home and Murray to second.

O'Brien was unnerved after the balk. Merkle crashed a double off the rightfield wall, scoring Murray. Herzog slammed one to the leftfield wall, scoring Merkle. Chief Meyers, one of the slowest men in the game, beat out a grounder to deep short.

With runners on first and third, McGraw tried to

double steal on the first pitch to Art Fletcher. The throw to second was wide, so Herzog scored and Meyers made it to third. McGraw then flashed the bunt sign. Fletcher laid down a beauty, and the Chief scooted across the plate.

"The noise that broke loose made all other demonstrations of the Series seem like whispers," reported *The New York Times*.

McGraw had given his men a pep talk before the game, and it seemed to have worked. Eight hitters. Six hits. Three stolen bases. Five runs.

A beaten Buck O'Brien was relieved by lefty Ray Collins. He shut out the Giants the rest of the game, but it was too late. Rube Marquard was mowing down the Red Sox hitters and the Giants defense was holding the ball tight for a change.

The final score was 5–2. A thousand Royal Rooters in attendance couldn't change that—though they did snake dance across the field after the game was over.

Many of the Red Sox felt the World Series would have been won right there if Smokey Joe Wood had been on the mound. Tempers flared on the train back to Boston. Wood's brother Paul socked Buck O'Brien, who brought a black eye back to Fenway.

The Sox were still in the driver's seat, though. They led the Series three games to two, and Smokey Joe Wood was rested and ready for Game 7.

Said John McGraw: "We will win the next two games and the Series."

GAME 7. It was a sunny morning, but by game time the sky had turned dark and blustery. The fans in Fenway were anxious for Boston to win this game and claim the world's championship. But the buzz in the stands was about what had happened the night before—former President Theodore Roosevelt had been shot and wounded by an insane assassin in Milwaukee.

Conversation stopped when the Royal Rooters entered the ballpark. Because of a ticket office mixup, their usual seats in the leftfield bleachers had been sold to the general public. The Rooters entered the ballpark to find *ordinary* fans already sitting in their seats and in no mood to leave. The Rooters were outraged.

Just as Smokey Joe Wood was walking to the mound to take his warm-up pitches, 500 Royal Rooters marched onto the field in protest. Honey Fitz and his brass band led the way. A half an hour of pushing, shoving, and fighting followed. Finally, police on horseback drove the Rooters off the field, but not before part of the outfield fence had been torn down.

By the time the field was clear, Joe Wood was stiff. The Giants leadoff batter, Josh Devore, hit a bouncer to short that Wagner booted. It was a sign of things to come.

Larry Doyle singled Devore to second, then the two of them pulled off a double steal. Runners on second and third, nobody out. A hitting barrage followed. Snodgrass doubled. Merkle singled. Meyers singled. Tesreau singled.

Balls were shooting off the Giants bats to all corners of Fenway Park.

When the rally was over, the Giants had put six runs across the plate. Wood had only thrown 13 pitches, but 7 of them had been socked for hits.

In the second inning, Charley Hall was brought in to relieve a battered Wood, but he wasn't much better. The Giants piled on another five runs. Doyle and Meyers each banged out 3 hits for the day, and the Giants had 16 as a team.

Giants pitcher Jeff Tesreau wasn't in top form, either. He walked 6 and allowed 19 Red Sox to reach first base. But only four of them scored, and the final score was Giants 11, Sox 4.

The tide had turned. Now the Series was even at three games apiece. The Giants had won two straight, and won them convincingly. They had momentum, and they had Christy Mathewson coming up to give one last try in the final, deciding game in Boston.

"In any race, if you can catch a man from behind you take the heart out of him," said John McGraw. "I believe that when we take the train for New York tomorrow night we will have the right to call ourselves the baseball champions of the world."

GAME 8. Fenway Park, Wednesday, October 16. After their seats had been sold for Game 7, the Royal Rooters decided to boycott Game 8. So did many other Bostonians. Only 17,034 people showed up for what would be one of the most famous baseball games ever played.

Those 17,000 fans made enough noise, though. Rattles had been handed out to every person entering the ballpark. When the rattles were banged against the seats, it sounded like "a chorus of giant crickets," according to *The New York Times*.

Christy Mathewson had said his career was over after losing Game 5, but there he was, warming up with renewed determination. Once again, Matty would be facing young Hugh Bedient, who had beaten him on Saturday. It would be another battle between youth and experience.

Before the game, manager Jake Stahl pulled Hugh Bedient aside and said, "Kid, you've got to win this one for us. It's the biggest game of your life. Just pitch the way you did your last time out and you can beat Mathewson."

Both teams were scoreless through two innings. Josh Devore walked on four pitches to lead off the Giants half of the third. Red Sox centerfielder Tris Speaker took a few steps forward. Speaker liked to play shallow, so he could snare bloops just beyond the infield. He could backtrack very quickly, and long fly balls rarely went over his head.

This was one time when it might have been a good idea for Speaker to play a little deeper. Red Murray whaled a long drive to left center. Speaker ran back and tipped the ball with his glove, but he couldn't hold on to it. As the ball rolled to the wall, Devore came around to score. Giants 1, Sox 0.

Other than that run, Bedient was working like an old pro. He didn't seem to be affected by the incredible pressure on him. Every few hitters, one of the Boston infielders would trot over and offer a few words of encouragement, but it didn't seem necessary. Bedient was in control, just as he had been in Game 5.

The Boston defense helped. In the sixth, Larry Doyle hit a drive to right center that looked like it was out of the park. Harry Hooper raced back and threw his body over a low railing into the second row of the stands. As fans propped him up, Hooper reached up and made an incredible catch. Some say it was bare-handed. It was another one of those plays people would call "the greatest catch ever made." We'll never know.

Mathewson was looking like the Matty of old—the Matty who had won 30 games a year from 1903 to 1905. Boston hitters couldn't get anything going against him—until the seventh inning.

With one out, Jake Stahl lifted a bloop into short left centerfield. Three Giants gave chase—shortstop Art Fletcher, leftfielder Red Murray, and centerfielder Fred Snodgrass. Each had the chance to make the play.

Nobody made the play. The ball dropped with a thud. Stahl was standing happily on second base. Rattled, Mathewson walked Heinie Wagner on four pitches. Runners on first and second, no outs.

It was Bedient's turn to bat, but Olaf Henriksen was sent up to pinch-hit for him. He was a rookie, but he had hit .321 during the regular season.

Mathewson and Henriksen had never faced each other before, and Matty quickly put two strikes past the rookie. Henriksen was looking lost out there. Mathewson threw a few pitches off the plate, but Henriksen refused to fish for them. Matty was going to have to put the ball in the strike zone.

He did, throwing his famous "fadeaway." But Henriksen wasn't fooled. He ripped a shot directly at third base. The ball nicked the bag and skittered foul. Stahl scored on the double, and it was Giants 1, Sox 1. Fenway Park erupted with cheers.

Nobody scored in the eighth or ninth. Smokey Joe Wood had been terrible the day before, but he was the best the Red Sox had, so he came in as a reliever. It was going to be Wood against Mathewson for the championship of the world, in extra innings.

With one out in the top of the tenth, Wood put one over the plate and Red Murray slammed it to left for a double. Fred Merkle hit the ball hard, too, a rocket right past Wood into centerfield. Murray respected Tris Speaker's throwing arm, but was determined to try and score anyway. Speaker picked up the ball in center as Murray was rounding third, but he bobbled it and Murray came around to score standing up. The Giants had the lead, 2–1.

Chief Meyers wanted to keep the rally alive. He hit a line drive up the middle, but Wood stopped it with his pitching hand and threw the Chief out at first to end the inning. Wood shook his hand in pain, and it was obvious that he was finished for the afternoon. It could be said that he got some good wood on the ball.

Now Christy Mathewson needed just three outs to bring the World Championship to New York. He looked confident.

Joe Wood's injury was a tough break for Boston. Wood was scheduled to lead off for the Red Sox in the bottom of the tenth, and he was a good hitter—.290 for the year. Boston had already used its best pinch hitter, Olaf Henriksen. They were forced to send up Clyde Engle—.234 for the season—to pinch-hit.

Engle made contact, a lazy fly ball to center. Giants rooters relaxed. Snodgrass could put that ball in his back pocket.

"I got it!" shouted Snodgrass. He drifted a few steps to his right and back.

Something happened. Snodgrass took his eye off the ball. He froze up. The pressure got to him. Something. The ball trickled off his glove and fell to the grass. The crowd let out a gasp. Engle was on second base.

"He hit a great big, lazy, high fly ball halfway between Red Murray in leftfield and me," Snodgrass told baseball historian Lawrence Ritter years later. "Murray called for it first, but as centerfielder I had preference over left and right, so there'd never be a collision. I yelled that I'd take it and waved Murray off, and—well—I dropped the darn thing."

It was a windy day, which made high flies difficult. But Snodgrass had no excuse. He should have had it. Christy Mathewson, known for being cool and calculating, looked stunned. Instead of one out and nobody on base, he had nobody out and the tying run in scoring position.

The top of the order was up for Boston. Harry Hooper. The Giants infield inched forward, looking for the bunt that would move Engle to third. Hooper squared around, but he tapped the ball foul.

Hooper took a full swing on the next pitch and hit it hard. It was a long drive to deep center, maybe a triple. Fred Snodgrass, feeling terrible about the last play, turned and ran back like a deer. He caught up with the ball near the wall and snared it over his shoulder. It was a spectacular play. Engle dashed back to second base, just beating the throw from Snodgrass.

One out. Two more and the Giants would be World Champions. They just had to prevent Engle from scoring.

Christy Mathewson was rattled by the Snodgrass error and Hooper's long drive. He walked Steve Yerkes, putting runners on first and second. A double play would end the Series, but the dangerous Tris Speaker was up. The crowd was screaming now, and it was almost impossible to hear anything else.

Mathewson threw a slow fadeaway on the inside corner. Speaker should have let the ball go by, but he took a weak swing and lofted a high pop up between home plate and first base. Again, Giants rooters breathed easy. It looked like the second out for sure.

First baseman Fred Merkle came in. Chief Meyers came out. Mathewson came over. Any of them could have made the play. The Boston bench, right next to the first baseline, screamed instructions meant to confuse the three Giants fielders.

"Chief! Chief! Chief!" yelled Matty.

Chief Meyers made a dive for it but just missed. The ball dropped a few feet foul near the first-base coach's box. Once again, the crowd gasped. "Anyone could have caught it," wrote sportswriter Hugh Fullerton. "I could have jumped out of the press box and caught it behind my back."

Now Mathewson was really steaming, making angry gestures as he yelled at Meyers and Merkle. Tris Speaker passed Mathewson on his way back to the batter's box and said, "You just called for the wrong man. It's gonna cost you this ball game."

True to his word, Speaker lined the next pitch into rightfield for a single. Engle came in to score the tying run. Yerkes stopped at third, and Speaker took second base on the throw home. The Giants were really in trouble. The run that could win the World Series for Boston was on third base. Duffy Lewis was striding to the plate, and he was dangerous.

McGraw decided to walk Lewis intentionally. That loaded the bases and set up a force play at any base.

Bottom of the tenth. Bases loaded. One out. 3–3 game. After struggling through 75 innings of the World Series, it all came down to this. A fly ball could win it all for Boston.

Larry Gardner was up. He had made two errors in the game and was looking to redeem himself. Matty needed a strikeout badly. If his teammates could only catch a baseball, he must have been thinking, he would be in the clubhouse shooting champagne by now.

Matty wheeled and dealt. The ball was over the plate, maybe a little high. Gardner swung and hit a fly ball to rightfield. Steve Yerkes got set to tag up from third after the catch.

Josh Devore caught the ball. Yerkes took off for the plate. Devore whipped the ball home with everything he had. The throw was on the money, but late. Yerkes trotted across the plate.

The Giants had been World Champions for nine and a half innings, but in six minutes they lost everything. The Boston Red Sox had won the World Series.

Fenway Park was in a frenzy. Red Sox fans took the field and cheered the players who had made it possible. Some shouted a special cheer for Fred Snodgrass, who had dropped the crucial fly ball.

Christy Mathewson and the Giants walked glumly off the field. Giants coach Wilbert Robinson collapsed in the dugout. New York sportswriter Sid Mercer had tears running down his cheeks as he dictated his story of the game. John McGraw went over to shake hands with Jake Stahl, and he was knocked over by a Red Sox fan.

The crowd sat in the ballpark for a half an hour. They couldn't believe it was all over.

The next morning, they paraded from Fenway Park to Faneuil Hall, tooting and singing every step of the way.

For Baseball Trivia Lovers . . .

♦ The New York Giants won the pennant for the third consecutive year in 1913. And for the third year in a row, they lost the World Series. The Red Sox won the Series again in 1915, 1916, and 1918, each time against a different National League team. In the 85 years since then, Boston hasn't won it once.

♦ A little-known member of the New York Giants in 1912 was Olympic decathlon champion Jim Thorpe. Thorpe won his medals that July, but they were taken away when it was discovered he had played a few professional baseball games. So John McGraw offered him $4,500 to play for the Giants, and Thorpe accepted.

He didn't appear in a game in 1912, while McGraw taught him the fine points of baseball. Over the next seven seasons, Thorpe compiled a .252 batting average, with 7 homers and 29 stolen bases. It has been said that Thorpe never made it as a baseball player because he couldn't hit the curveball.

♦ Smokey Joe Wood broke his thumb the next spring and his career as a pitcher went downhill. But he was such a good hitter that he switched to the outfield, where he compiled a lifetime .283 batting average before retiring after the 1922 season. He coached at Yale for 20 years. Wood died in 1985.

The first professional baseball Smokey Joe played was with the Bloomer Girls, an all-female team. Over the years they hired a number of men to play for the team, frequently wearing wigs so fans would think they were women. Hall of Famer Rogers Hornsby was also a Bloomer Girl.

Wood's son, also named Joe, became a ballplayer, too. But he wasn't nearly as good as his dad. Pitching for Boston in 1944, Joe, Jr., only appeared in three major league games. He was tagged for 13 hits in nine innings and was out of baseball forever.

♦ Two years after this World Series, the Red Sox picked up another young pitcher who was turned into a hitter—Babe Ruth.

♦ Rube Marquard and Smokey Joe Wood were born 16 days apart, in 1889. If Marquard was playing under today's rules, he would have won 20 straight games instead of 19. He was a relief pitcher for one game. The Giants came from behind to win, but the victory was credited to the starting pitcher.

♦ Christy Mathewson's career wasn't finished in 1912 after all. He came back to win 25 games in 1913 and 24 in 1914. He retired in 1916 and became the manager of the Cincinnati Reds.

♦ The Red Sox players each earned $4,025 for winning the World Series; the Giants earned $2,566. In those days, most players didn't make $4,000 all *season*, and working people considered that much money a small fortune.

♦ Fred Snodgrass's muffed fly ball in the tenth inning of the final game became one of the most famous errors in baseball history. The difference between the winning team's share and the losing team's share was around $30,000, and Snodgrass's error came to be called the "$30,000 muff." Sportswriter Fred Lieb, who accompanied the Giants on their train home after the Series, said that Snodgrass "sat like a man in a trance, his eyes glued to the window."

When he passed away 62 years later, *The New York Times* summed up his life with this headline: FRED SNODGRASS, 86, DEAD; BALL PLAYER MUFFED 1912 FLY

♦ The error Snodgrass made was one of 31 errors committed during the 1912 World Series.

♦ In those days, baseball players had the reputation of being uneducated rowdies, but many of the participants in this World Series were college educated: Jake Stahl (University of Illinois), Steve Yerkes (University of Pennsylvania), Buck Herzog (University of Maryland), Larry Gardner and Ray Collins (University of Vermont), Harry Hooper and Duffy Lewis (St. Mary's), Chief

Meyers (Dartmouth), Bill Carrigan (Holy Cross), Christy Mathewson (Bucknell), and John McGraw (St. Bonaventure).

◆ President William Howard Taft started two baseball traditions: Throwing out the first ball to start the season, and the seventh-inning stretch. The story goes that Taft was at the ballpark one day, and toward the end of the game he stood up to stretch his legs. The crowd thought the president was leaving, so they respectfully stood up. But then Taft sat down to enjoy the rest of the game, and so did everybody else.

◆ In the eighth inning of Game 7, Boston centerfielder Tris Speaker pulled off a rare unassisted double play. He grabbed a short fly and ran across second base before the Giant baserunner could get back to the bag.

◆ After the World Series, the *Spalding Guide* wrote, "No individual, whether player, manager, owner, critic or spectator who went through the 1912 World Series will ever forget it." *The New York Times* called the ending, "the most stirring finish of a world championship in the history of baseball."

But then, that was just 1912. Read on.

BOX SCORES

Game 1
Tuesday, October 8, At New York

Boston	AB.	R.	H.	RBI.	PO.	A.
Hooper, rf	3	1	1	1	1	0
Yerkes, 2b	4	0	1	2	0	1
Speaker, cf	3	1	0	0	1	0
Lewis, lf	4	0	0	1	2	0
Gardner, 3b	4	0	0	0	1	1
Stahl, 1b	4	0	0	0	6	1
Wagner, ss	3	1	2	0	5	3
Cady, c	3	0	1	0	11	1
Wood, p	3	1	0	0	1	1
Totals	31	4	6	4	27	9

New York	AB.	R.	H.	RBI.	PO.	A.
Devore, lf	3	1	0	0	0	0
Doyle, 2b	4	1	2	0	2	7
Snodgrass, cf	4	0	1	0	2	0
Murray, rf	3	0	1	2	1	0
Merkle, 1b	4	1	1	0	12	0
Herzog, 3b	4	0	2	0	1	1
Meyers, c	3	0	1	1	6	1
bBecker	0	0	0	0	0	0
Fletcher, ss	4	0	0	0	3	1
Tesreau, p	4	0	0	0	2	2
aMcCormick	1	0	0	0	0	0
Crandall, p	1	0	0	0	0	1
Totals	33	3	8	3	27	13

Boston	0 0 0	0 0 1	3 0 0—4
New York	0 0 2	0 0 0	0 0 1—3

Boston	IP.	H.	R.	ER.	BB.	SO.
Wood (W)	9	8	3	3	2	11

New York	IP.	H.	R.	ER.	BB.	SO.
Tesreau (L)	7	5	4	4	4	4
Crandall	2	1	0	0	0	2

Game 2
Wednesday, October 9, At Boston

New York	AB.	R.	H.	RBI.	PO.	A.
Snodgrass, lf-rf	4	1	1	0	0	0
Doyle, 2b	5	0	1	0	2	5
Becker, rf	4	1	0	0	0	1
Murray, rf-lf	5	2	3	2	3	0
Merkle, 1b	5	1	1	0	19	0
Herzog, 3b	4	1	3	2	2	4
Meyers, c	4	0	2	1	5	0
aShafer, ss	0	0	0	0	0	3
Fletcher, ss	4	0	0	0	1	3
bMcCormick	0	0	0	1	0	0
Wilson, c	0	0	0	0	0	1
Mathewson, p	5	0	0	0	1	6
Totals	40	6	11	6	33	23

Boston	AB.	R.	H.	RBI.	PO.	A.
Hooper, rf	5	1	3	0	3	0
Yerkes, 2b	5	1	1	1	3	4
Speaker, cf	5	2	2	0	2	0
Lewis, lf	5	2	2	0	2	0
Gardner, 3b	4	0	0	1	2	0
Stahl, 1b	5	0	2	2	10	0
Wagner, ss	5	0	0	0	5	5
Carrigan, c	5	0	0	0	6	4
Collins, p	3	0	0	0	0	1
Hall, p	1	0	0	0	0	0
Bedient, p	1	0	0	0	0	0
Totals	44	6	10	4	33	14

New York	0 1 0	1 0 0	0 3 0	1 0—6
Boston	3 0 0	0 1 0	0 1 0	1 0—6

(Game called at end of 11th inning on account of darkness.)

New York	IP.	H.	R.	ER.	BB.	SO.
Mathewson	11	10	6	2	0	4

Boston	IP.	H.	R.	ER.	BB.	SO.
Collins	7⅓	9	5	3	0	5
Hall	2⅓	2	1	1	4	0
Bedient	1	0	0	0	1	1

Game 3
Thursday, October 10, At Boston

New York	AB.	R.	H.	RBI.	PO.	A.
Devore, rf	4	0	2	0	2	0
Doyle, 2b	3	0	0	0	3	1
Snodgrass, cf	4	0	1	0	0	0
Murray, lf	4	1	1	0	5	0
Merkle, 1b	3	0	0	0	5	0
Herzog, 3b	2	1	1	1	1	3
Meyers, c	4	0	1	0	8	1
Fletcher, ss	3	0	1	1	0	2
Marquard, p	1	0	0	0	0	2
Totals	28	2	7	2	27	9

Boston	AB.	R.	H.	RBI.	PO.	A.
Hooper, rf	3	0	0	0	1	0
Yerkes, 2b	4	0	1	0	3	1
Speaker, cf	4	0	1	0	3	1
Lewis, lf	4	1	2	0	4	0
Gardner, 3b	3	0	1	1	0	2
Stahl, 1b	4	0	2	0	11	1
cHenriksen	0	0	0	0	0	0
Wagner, ss	4	0	0	1	3	3
Carrigan, c	2	0	0	0	3	1
aEngle	1	0	0	0	0	0
O'Brien, p	2	0	0	0	1	5
bBall	1	0	0	0	0	0
Cady, c	1	0	0	0	0	1
Bedient, p	0	0	0	0	0	0
Totals	33	1	7	1	27	15

New York	0 1 0	0 1 0	0 0 0—2
Boston	0 0 0	0 0 0	0 0 1—1

New York	IP.	H.	R.	ER.	BB.	SO.
Marquard (W)	9	7	1	1	1	6

Boston	IP.	H.	R.	ER.	BB.	SO.
O'Brien (L)	8	6	2	2	3	3
Bedient	1	1	0	0	0	0

Game 4
Friday, October 11, At New York

Boston	AB.	R.	H.	RBI.	PO.	A.
Hooper, rf	4	0	1	0	1	0
Yerkes, 2b	3	0	1	0	2	5
Speaker, cf	4	0	1	0	0	0
Lewis, lf	4	0	0	0	1	0
Gardner, 3b	3	2	2	0	0	2
Stahl, 1b	3	1	0	0	9	0
Wagner, ss	3	0	0	0	2	3
Cady, c	4	0	1	1	10	0
Wood, p	4	0	2	1	1	2
Totals	32	3	8	2	27	12

New York	AB.	R.	H.	RBI.	PO.	A.
Devore, lf	4	0	1	0	0	0
Doyle, 2b	4	1	0	1	4	1
Snodgrass, cf	4	0	0	2	0	0
Murray, rf	4	0	1	0	3	0
Merkle, 1b	4	0	1	0	8	0
Herzog, 3b	4	1	2	0	2	1
Meyers, c	4	0	0	0	5	1
Fletcher, ss	4	0	1	1	3	0
Tesreau, p	2	0	1	0	0	2
aMcCormick	1	0	1	0	0	0
Ames, p	0	0	0	0	0	0
Totals	35	1	9	1	27	12

Boston	0 1 0	1 0 0	0 0 1—3
New York	0 0 0	0 0 0	1 0 0—1

Boston	IP.	H.	R.	ER.	BB.	SO.
Wood (W)	9	9	1	1	0	8

New York	IP.	H.	R.	ER.	BB.	SO.
Tesreau (L)	7	5	2	2	2	5
Ames	2	3	1	1	0	0

BOX SCORES

Game 5

New York	AB.	R.	H.	RBI.	PO.	A.
Devore, lf	2	0	0	0	0	0
Doyle, 2b	4	0	0	0	0	3
Snodgrass, cf	4	0	0	0	2	0
Murray, rf	3	0	0	0	0	1
Merkle, 1b	4	1	1	1	15	0
Herzog, 3b	4	0	0	0	2	3
Meyers, c	3	0	1	0	2	0
Fletcher, ss	2	0	0	0	2	2
aMcCormick	1	0	0	0	0	0
bShafer, ss	0	0	0	0	1	1
Mathewson, p	3	0	1	0	0	3
Totals	30	1	3	0	24	13

Boston	AB.	R.	H.	RBI.	PO.	A.
Hooper, rf	4	1	2	0	4	0
Yerkes, 2b	4	1	1	1	3	3
Speaker, cf	3	0	1	1	3	0
Lewis, lf	3	0	0	0	1	0
Gardner, 3b	3	0	0	0	3	2
Stahl, 1b	3	0	0	0	7	0
Wagner, ss	3	0	1	0	1	1
Cady, c	3	0	0	0	5	0
Bedient, p	3	0	0	0	0	0
Totals	29	2	5	2	27	6

New York .... 0 0 0 0 0 0 1 0 0—1
Boston .... 0 0 2 0 0 0 0 0 x—2

New York	IP.	H.	R.	ER.	BB.	SO.
Mathewson (L)	8	5	2	2	0	2

Boston	IP.	H.	R.	ER.	BB.	SO.
Bedient (W)	9	3	1	0	3	4

Game 6

Boston	AB.	R.	H.	RBI.	PO.	A.
Hooper, rf	4	0	1	0	2	2
Yerkes, 2b	4	0	2	0	3	1
Speaker, cf	3	0	0	0	5	0
Lewis, lf	4	0	0	0	0	0
Gardner, 3b	4	1	0	0	0	1
Stahl, 1b	4	1	2	0	8	0
Wagner, ss	4	0	0	0	3	0
Cady, c	3	0	1	0	3	2
O'Brien, p	0	0	0	0	0	1
aEngle	1	0	1	2	0	0
Collins, p	0	0	0	0	0	0
Totals	31	2	7	2	24	9

New York	AB.	R.	H.	RBI.	PO.	A.
Devore, rf	4	0	1	0	2	0
Doyle, 2b	4	1	1	0	1	1
Snodgrass, cf	4	0	1	0	6	0
Murray, rf	3	1	1	1	0	0
Merkle, 1b	3	1	2	1	4	1
Herzog, 3b	3	1	1	0	0	1
Meyers, c	3	1	2	0	6	0
Fletcher, ss	3	0	1	0	2	2
Marquard, p	3	0	0	0	2	2
Totals	30	5	11	3	27	7

Boston .... 0 2 0 0 0 0 0 0 0—2
New York .... 1 5 0 0 0 0 0 0 x—5

Boston	IP.	H.	R.	ER.	BB.	SO.
O'Brien (L)	1	6	5	3	0	1
Collins	7	5	0	0	0	1

New York	IP.	H.	R.	ER.	BB.	SO.
Marquard (W)	9	7	2	0	1	3

Game 7

New York	AB.	R.	H.	RBI.	PO.	A.
Devore, rf	4	2	1	0	3	1
Doyle, 2b	4	3	3	2	3	3
Snodgrass, cf	5	1	2	2	1	0
Murray, lf	4	0	0	1	0	0
Merkle, 1b	5	1	2	1	10	0
Herzog, 3b	4	2	1	0	0	2
Meyers, c	4	1	3	1	6	0
Wilson, c	1	0	1	0	2	0
Fletcher, ss	5	1	2	1	2	4
Tesreau, p	4	0	2	2	0	6
Totals	40	11	16	8	27	16

Boston	AB.	R.	H.	RBI.	PO.	A.
Hooper, rf	3	0	1	1	1	1
Yerkes, 2b	4	0	0	0	1	4
Speaker, cf	4	1	1	0	4	0
Lewis, lf	4	1	1	1	3	0
Gardner, 3b	4	1	1	1	2	0
Stahl, 1b	5	0	1	0	11	1
Wagner, ss	5	0	1	0	4	4
Cady, c	4	1	0	0	1	2
Wood, p	0	0	0	0	0	1
Hall, p	3	0	3	0	0	5
Totals	36	4	9	3	27	18

New York .... 6 1 0 0 0 2 1 0 1—11
Boston .... 0 1 0 0 0 0 2 1 0—4

New York	IP.	H.	R.	ER.	BB.	SO.
Tesreau (W)	9	9	4	2	5	6

Boston	IP.	H.	R.	ER.	BB.	SO.
Wood (L)	1	7	6	4	0	0
Hall	8	9	5	3	5	1

Game 8

New York	AB.	R.	H.	RBI.	PO.	A.
Devore, rf	3	1	1	0	3	1
Doyle, 2b	5	0	0	0	5	5
Snodgrass, cf	4	0	1	0	4	1
Murray, lf	5	1	2	1	3	0
Merkle, 1b	5	0	1	1	10	0
Herzog, 3b	5	0	2	0	2	1
Meyers, c	3	0	1	0	4	3
Fletcher, ss	3	0	1	0	2	4
bMcCormick	1	0	0	0	0	0
Shafer, ss	0	0	0	0	0	0
Mathewson, p	4	0	0	0	2	0
Totals	38	2	9	2	29	15

Boston	AB.	R.	H.	RBI.	PO.	A.
Hooper, rf	5	0	0	0	3	0
Yerkes, 2b	4	1	1	0	0	3
Speaker, cf	4	0	2	1	2	0
Lewis, lf	4	0	0	0	1	0
Gardner, 3b	3	0	1	1	1	4
Stahl, 1b	4	1	2	0	15	0
Wagner, ss	3	0	1	0	3	5
Cady, c	4	0	0	0	5	3
Bedient, p	2	0	0	0	0	0
aHenriksen	1	1	1	1	0	0
Wood, p	0	0	0	0	0	2
cEngle	1	0	0	0	0	0
Totals	35	3	8	3	30	18

New York .... 0 0 1 0 0 0 0 0 0 1—2
Boston .... 0 0 0 0 0 0 1 0 0 2—3

Two out when winning run scored.

New York	IP.	H.	R.	ER.	BB.	SO.
Mathewson (L)	9⅔	8	3	1	5	4

Boston	IP.	H.	R.	ER.	BB.	SO.
Bedient	7	6	1	1	3	2
Wood (W)	3	3	1	1	1	2

CHAPTER

2

1924

Washington Senators

vs.

New York Giants

Last Chance to Be the Hero

Giants catcher Hank Gowdy went back for a foul pop and got his foot caught in his own catcher's mask. He couldn't have picked a worse possible time. (NBL)

...WIN WORLD CHAMPIONSHIP,
N PITCHING THEM TO VICTORY
GIANTS, 4 TO 3, IN 12-INNING BATTLE

Coolidge Joins in Ce
brating Washington'
First Baseball Title.

JOHNSON TO THE RESC

Over Senators' Victory;
ohnson i

CAPITAL WILD WITH JOY

Called in Ninth, He Holds N
York at Bay While Team
Vinning Blows

ET A REC

igures, Howe
the Only Othe
ollar Series.

New York Times
Oct. 10.—In the
Senators won.
baseball that
tortured their pe
They beat the G
nt today, 4 to 3,
came to the capit
and the "breaks
victory in the twe
New York cat
mask and droppe
ckson fumbled an
muff Ruel hit a
the fumble Eas
As the ball le
head and rolled
le Napoleon me

aseball drama, b
e people's team
re triumphed over
of a great bas
s slowly grinding
In the last act W
a tired old man,
down before a
e great Kansas
eyville Cyclone
fast that other

This photo, found in the files of the Baseball Hall of Fame, is one of the only action shots of the 1924 World Series. Numbers did not appear on uniforms at the time, and it is impossible to identify the people in this play at the plate. (NBL)

game of champion
ayed in this cou
self. If Walter J
son went back to 1912, so did Joh
McGraw. Tonight he must be thir
of that other seven-game series,
in the twelfth inning a fielder dro
a fly and another failed to catch a
and the Red Sox went on to win. It
McGraw's turn in the twelfth in
today, but for the second time in tw
years the fortunes of the game
against him.

Luck of Game Decisive.

Here was a game that hung on
roll of a ball or the twist of a
In years to come they will call, Go
failure the $50,000 muff and Judg
misplay the $50,000 fumble. But it
not Gowdy nor Jackson who decided
game. It was not McNeely nor
nor Harris who won it. Not the
ators but the luck of the play
the Giants.
Washington, a city gone mad ton

AGA
N WI'
SENA'

Title in Their Grasp
of Sixth Game in
pital Today,

ITS OFF VETERAN

ocks a Homer, While
uals Ruth's Record
Circuit Blows.

BEATING GIANTS, 4-3,
TO PLAY HERE TODAY

Peckinpaugh's Double In Stirring Ninth With Score Tied

GIANTS DEFEAT SEN
40,000, INCLUDING COOLIDGE, SEE
LOSE A THRILLING 12-INNING

EIGHTEEN-YEAR-OLD Walter Johnson was a telephone repairman in Idaho in 1905. A traveling salesman from Washington saw him pitch for a semipro team one day and sent this note to the manager of the Washington Senators:

"This boy throws so fast you can't see 'em. And he knows where he is throwing, because if he didn't there would be dead bodies all over Idaho."

It was true. Johnson had a loose, easy sidearm motion, but the ball rocketed from his hand like it had been shot from a gun. His long right arm was like a whip. Catchers were afraid to catch him. Hitters were terrified. Even Johnson *himself* was afraid of his own fastball—afraid he was going to kill someone with it.*

Johnson didn't bother much with a curveball. Didn't have to.

The Washington Senators sent an injured catcher named Cliff Blankenship to Idaho to take a look at the young speed demon. Blankenship wasn't expecting much, but when he saw Johnson with his own eyes he knew he was seeing one of the greatest right arms ever.

The Senators offered Johnson $100 to sign with the team. To a farm boy in Idaho, that must have seemed like all the money in the world. So Walter Johnson signed his first contract on a piece of brown wrapping

---

*Legend has it that Walter Johnson was afraid to pitch batters inside. But the record shows that he hit 206 batters, more than any pitcher in baseball history.

paper. He boarded a train and headed for the nation's capital.

Johnson only won five games his first season, but in 1910 he won 25 and posted an earned run average of 1.35. He struck out an astonishing 313 batters while walking only 76. He was a phenomenon that came to be called the Big Train. He was also an authentic American hero who didn't smoke, drink, or get in trouble.

Johnson went on to win 20 or more games the next ten seasons in a row. In 1912 he won 16 straight games and 32 all together. The next year his record was an unbeliev-able 36–7 with a 1.09 ERA. He pitched 12 shutouts that year, and 5 of them were one-hitters.

What was even *more* remarkable, Walter Johnson played for the worst team in baseball. In Johnson's first 13 years, the Senators finished in seventh place or worse nine times. They hadn't won a pennant since entering the league in 1901.

The line about Washington was: "First in war, first in peace, and last in the American League."

In 1923, the lowly Senators finished 24 games out of first place. By then, Walter Johnson was 36 years old and nearing the end of his career. His fastball wasn't so fast anymore. He had always dreamed of winning a World Series game, but it looked like it would never happen. After 18 years in the big leagues, Johnson announced that 1924 would be his last season.

But Walter Johnson went out with a bang. He led the

league in wins (23), shutouts (6), winning percentage (.767), strikeouts (158), and ERA (2.72) Johnson won 13 straight games, and, as if it were destiny, the Washington Senators won their first pennant on the last weekend of the 1924 season.

This was the year the Senators finally came together as a team. Joe Judge played a smooth first base and hit .324. Roger Peckinpaugh (.272) at short, and Ossie Bluege (pronounced *Blu-gee*) at third formed one of baseball's tightest infields. The outfield was a hitting machine with Goose Goslin (.344) in left, Sam Rice (.334) in right and Earl McNeely (.330) in center. Catcher Muddy Ruel weighed just 135 pounds, but he was tough as nails and hit .283.

They were a good team, but not a great team. All the Senators put together hit only 22 home runs, and Goslin hit 12 of them. The pitching staff wasn't anything to rave about, but every fourth day they had Walter Johnson on the mound.

And they had one extra ingredient no other team possessed—a burning desire to win a pennant for the Old Man, as Johnson was called.

You may have noticed that there's no second baseman above. Second base was played by Bucky Harris, who also was the manager of the Senators. Harris had left school at 13 to work in the coal mines of Pennsylvania. Thanks to his talent at baseball, he went from being a miner to the majors.

Harris was just 27 years old in 1924 and managing for the first time. He was called the Boy Wonder.

THE NEW YORK GIANTS were almost the direct opposite of the Washington Senators. They were a powerhouse, winning their eighth National League pennant in 14 years, and their fourth in a row. Four of their hitters slugged ten or more homers. Their manager, John McGraw, had been the leader of the Giants for 22 years.

The only veteran in the Giants infield was switch-hitter Frank Frisch, who hit .328 and hardly ever struck out. But he would be playing the World Series hurt. He had a sprained finger on his right hand, and just before Game 1 he accidentally slammed his other hand in a car door. The other infielders were rookies Travis Jackson (.302) at short, Bill Terry (.239) at first, and Fred Lindstrom (.253) at third.

Lindstrom was a particularly raw rookie. He had been plucked out of high school in Chicago early, and was the starting third baseman in the World Series at the age of 18. Lindstrom was an infant when Walter Johnson pitched his first major league game.

John McGraw played some platooning games with lefties and righties in his lineup, which would play an important role in this World Series, as we will see. His outfield was patrolled by Pep Youngs (.356), rookie Hack Wilson (.295), Irish Meusel (.310), and George "Highpockets" Kelly (.324). Kelly hit 21 home runs during the season—one less than the entire Senators team.

The Giants catcher was Hank Gowdy (.325), who would make a play that would turn this World Series upside down.

GAME 1. It was warm for an October day in Washington. The sky was overcast. But the capital had never hosted a World Series, and 36,000 fans filled every seat in Griffith Stadium. An extra 18 rows had been added in the outfield, which shortened the fences and would make home runs plentiful. Reserved seats sold for $3.30, and bleachers for $1.10. Scalpers on Pennsylvania Avenue were getting as much as $75 a ticket.

A few hundred people paid 50 cents each to stand on the roofs of four houses overlooking centerfield. There were even a few diehard fans clinging to telegraph poles surrounding the ballpark. They would have been better off finding a radio. Baseball had been broadcast by radio for the first time three years earlier, and this was one of the first World Series that could be heard live.

Before the game the fans of Washington presented Walter Johnson with a green Lincoln automobile to show their appreciation for all his effort over the years. Everyone in America—with the possible exception of Giants fans—was rooting for Johnson and the Senators. Every time he would come to bat, walk to the dugout, or strike somebody out in this game, the Big Train would be cheered wildly by the crowd.

A few minutes before two o'clock, cheers poured out of the stands even though Johnson hadn't done a thing. The president of the United States, Calvin Coolidge, and his wife, Grace, made their way down the aisle. They were seated in a flag-draped box near the Washington dugout.

Grace Coolidge enjoys a good laugh while President Coolidge throws out the first ball. The president only attended baseball games to win votes. It was Mrs. Coolidge who was the diehard Senators fan. (Library of Congress)

Coolidge wasn't much of a baseball fan, but he was up for reelection in a month, and it wouldn't hurt to be seen presiding over the World Series. Grace Coolidge was the real fan in the family. She carefully scored the game with her scorecard and jumped from her seat and shouted any time something good happened for the Senators. The president only clapped his hands mechanically.

Babe Ruth and Ty Cobb, whose teams hadn't reached the World Series, came over to chat with Calvin Coolidge. A chubby boy in white flannel pants handed the president a ball and said, "Please sign it; it may give us good luck." Coolidge signed the ball.

A military band played "The Star-Spangled Banner." Washington manager Bucky Harris handed the president a baseball, and Coolidge threw it wild and high to umpire Tommy Connolly. The ump made a leaping, bare-handed grab. The next day the newspapers called it the best play of the day.

On the pitcher's mound, Walter Johnson pulled the belt around his waist, as he always did. He put the ball down and picked up some dirt in his hand. He rolled the dirt between his forefinger and his thumb. Then he picked up the ball again, wound up, and threw it.

Ball one, outside. The 1924 World Series was under way.

Johnson handled the Giants easily in the first inning. When he struck out Pep Youngs for the third out, a hat sailed out of the stands and onto the field.

On the mound for the Giants was lefthander Art Nehf. He wasn't any Walter Johnson, but he'd won 21, 20, and 19 games in 1920–1922. And unlike Johnson, Nehf had World Series experience. He pitched complete game victories to win the finales of the Series in 1921 and 1922.

After the first inning, things got rocky for the Big Train. In the second, he had a full count on George Kelly when Kelly ripped a shot to left. Goose Goslin fell backwards over the low bleacher wall trying to catch it, but it was no use. Home run. Giants 1, Senators 0.

In the fourth inning, Bill Terry got hold of a Johnson fastball and whaled it into the leftfield bleachers. Giants 2, Senators 0. Gloom hung over the ballpark. Maybe Johnson *was* over the hill.

Meanwhile, Giants lefthander Art Nehf had a no-hitter through three innings and a shutout through five. But Washington centerfielder Earl McNeely led off the sixth with a double down the leftfield line. He took third on a ground out.

Sam Rice was up. A dozen years earlier, Rice suffered a terrible personal tragedy when a tornado in Illinois killed his wife, his two children, and his parents. Rice was in the minors at the time. He went on to survive the trauma and have a Hall of Fame career. This season he led the league with 216 hits.

Rice crowded the plate and stood erect in the batter's box. He tapped a slow roller to third. Fred Lindstrom made the play to first, but McNeely scored and Washington had its first World Series run.

Giants 2, Senators 1. That's the way it stayed going into the bottom of the ninth. New York needed three outs to wrap up Game 1. Nehf and Johnson were still the pitchers of record.

Ossie Bluege, who worked as an accountant during the off season, was first up for the Senators. He slapped a grounder to short. Giants shortstop Travis Jackson had led the league in errors, and true to form the ball ticked off his glove for an infield hit. Runner on first, nobody out.

Roger Peckinpaugh was up. Nehf delivered, and Peck drove the ball off the leftfield wall. Bleuge came all the way around to score and Peck was standing on second. Giants 2, Senators 2.

The people of Washington had waited nearly a quarter century to have something to cheer about, and they went absolutely crazy. Dozens of seat cushions, hats, gloves, and even coats sailed out of the stands. A crumpled newspaper fell from the upper deck and bounced off President Coolidge's head, knocking his hat askew.

It was five minutes before the game could resume. During the delay, the president decided he'd had enough of baseball for the day. He stood up and prepared to leave.

"Where do you think you're going?" barked Grace Coolidge as she grabbed the president's coattails. "You sit down."

The president returned to his seat.

Art Nehf prevented any further scoring in the ninth inning. He and Walter Johnson were two determined pitchers. Neither team could push a run across the plate in the tenth or eleventh innings.

Johnson walked Giants catcher Hank Gowdy to start the twelfth, with ball four hitting Gowdy on the shoulder. Art Nehf was up. It was a pinch-hitting situation, but Nehf already had two hits off Johnson, so he was sent up to the plate.

Nehf hit a high fly to short centerfield. Earl McNeely dashed in and snatched it at his shoetops, but then fell and the ball dropped out of his glove. That put runners at second and third with nobody out.

Walter Johnson was looking nervous. He walked pinch hitter Jack Bentley on four pitches to load the bases. Gowdy, not the fastest runner, was at third.

Frank Frisch, the Fordham Flash, was up. He slapped a grounder up the middle. Gowdy chugged for the plate. Bucky Harris dashed over and gloved the ball. He wheeled and threw home.

Out! The great play by Harris prevented the go-ahead run from scoring. The bases were still loaded. One out.

Lefty Pep Youngs was up. He was scheduled to be married on Friday night and he must have been nervous about it. He'd already struck out three times in the game. But this time he got enough bat on a Johnson fastball to bloop it into centerfield. Art Nehf scored and the Giants were in front again, 3–2.

When George Kelly hit a long fly ball to score another run, Griffith Stadium sounded like a tomb. Going into the bottom of the twelfth, it was Giants 4, Senators 2.

Walter Johnson was scheduled to lead off for the Senators, and Mule Shirley was sent up to pinch hit for him. He hit a pop fly to deep short. Jackson drifted back and muffed it, his second boot of the game. Mule made it to second base.

The crowd was screaming for a hit, and Bucky Harris delivered a single that scored Shirley. Now it was Giants 4, Senators 3. The tying run was on first.

When Sam Rice whacked a single up the middle, pandemonium took over the crowd. But Rice, in his excitement, tried to stretch his single into a double. He was out by a mile.

It was a stupid blunder. If Rice had stayed at first base, the Senators would have had runners at first and third with one out. Goose Goslin, who led the league in RBIs, was coming up. It would have been a cinch to bring the tying run home. By losing such a gamble, there were two outs, making it harder to score from third.

That became obvious when Goslin hit a smash to the right side of the infield. Harris raced from third base for the plate, but first baseman Kelly bare-handed the ball, wheeled, and threw it to Nehf to end the game.

"It was the most thrilling and best-played game I have ever watched," said President Coolidge, not all that convincingly.

In a corner of the Washington clubhouse Walter Johnson sat, his shoulders drooping with fatigue. He had pitched the full 12 innings and struck out a dozen Giants to set a World Series record. But the capital L in the box score next to his name told the real story. He was the losing pitcher.

"I gave them everything I had, and it wasn't good enough," he said. "I'm tired—you bet I'm tired. But I'll be all right again in a little while, and I'm ready to go back in there."

The reporter noted that Johnson's lower lip quivered with emotion as he talked. Walter Johnson had to be thinking that he might get just one more chance to win a World Series game. And Washington fans had to be thinking that if the great Walter Johnson couldn't beat the New York Giants, who could?

GAME 2. The opening ceremonies were over, and the nation's capital settled in for the business of determining the World Championship. President and Mrs. Coolidge didn't attend Game 2, though inning-by-inning reports were flashed by radio to the president's yacht *Mayflower* in Chesapeake Bay.

Two lefthanders went at it this Sunday afternoon. For the Senators, it was Tom Zachary. His jerky delivery had won 15 games for Washington.

Jack Bentley, also a 15-game winner, was on the hill for the Giants. Bentley was actually a better hitter than a pitcher. He averaged .291 lifetime, and in 1923 he hit .427. Some called him the next Babe Ruth.

Washington struck first. With two out in the bottom of the first inning, Sam Rice singled and stole second. Bentley had a full count on Goose Goslin, and Goose pulled the next pitch into the rightfield bleachers. Senators 2, Giants 0.

Field captains Frank Frisch of the Giants and Bucky Harris of the Senators shake hands and come out fighting. (NBL)

After the game Washington manager Bucky Harris would say, "I've seen a lot of nice things in Washington—the White House, the Capitol, the Washington Monument. But I never enjoyed any sight as much as I did watching that ball of Goslin's sail into the bleachers."

Jack Bentley was pitching well for the Giants, but one or two mistakes can kill you. In the fifth inning, Bucky Harris took him over the wall. Harris's homer made the score 3–0 in favor of the Senators.

Meanwhile, Tom Zachary was cruising. After escaping from a bases-loaded jam in the first inning, he retired the side in order in the second, third, and fifth. Zachary hadn't struck out a single Giant, but he was working on a three-hitter through the sixth inning. He gave up a run in the seventh, but Zachary was in command. Senators 3, Giants 1.

When Babe Ruth and Ty Cobb failed to stand up for the traditional seventh-inning stretch, fans jeered the two superstars. A woman got up to leave during the eighth inning and the fans around her *really* let her have it. Shamefaced, she returned to her seat and stayed for the rest of the game.

Going into the ninth inning, Washington clung to their 3–1 lead. But Tom Zachary walked Giants leadoff hitter Frank Frisch on four pitches. Zachary got an out when Pep Youngs popped to short. But with Frisch running on the 3–2 pitch, George Kelly cracked a long single to right center.

Frank Frisch didn't stop at second, and he didn't stop at third either. He was determined to score. The throw to the plate came in high. By the time Senators catcher Muddy Ruel slapped the tag on Frisch's chest, the Fordham Flash was already across the plate. The Senators argued the call, but the score was 3–2, and the Giants were hungry for more.

Irish Meusel was up for New York. (He wasn't really Irish; he just looked Irish.) He slapped a grounder up the middle. Bucky Harris made a great play getting to the ball and threw Meusel out at first. George Kelly, who represented the tying run, advanced to second on the play.

Two outs now, and Hack Wilson took his place in the batter's box. Wilson, a future Hall of Famer, was a rookie in 1924. With the count two balls and two strikes, he lined a single to right.

Kelly rounded third and headed home.

Sam Rice grabbed the bouncing ball in rightfield. There would be a play at the plate.

Rice's throw was ahead of the runner, but catcher Muddy Ruel bobbled the ball for a moment.

Kelly dove for the plate, colliding with Ruel.

Safe! The game was tied at 3–3.

Washington fans were disheartened, but perked up when Joe Judge walked to lead off the bottom of the ninth. The game-winning run was on. The Giants infield gathered around Jack Bentley to offer words of encouragement.

Ossie Bluege was instructed to bunt Judge to second, and he laid down Bentley's first pitch perfectly. The winning run was now in scoring position with one out. Roger Peckinpaugh walked up to the plate swinging two bats.

It was Peck who tied up Game 1 in the ninth with a timely double. New York manager John McGraw thought about walking him intentionally, but decided the odds were against Peck coming through in the clutch two days in a row.

Bentley threw the first pitch out of the strike zone and Peck watched it go by. He fouled off the next one to even the count. Bentley followed with a fastball. Peck liked it and ripped it down the third-base line.

Fred Lindstrom made a dive for the ball, but it was past him even before he left his feet. Joe Judge scooted around third and the fans of Washington shrieked with joy as he crossed the plate.

Game over! Senators 4, Giants 3. The World Series was tied at one game apiece.

In all the excitement, few noticed that Roger Peckinpaugh grabbed his left leg in pain as he ran to first after his game-winning hit. He had severely pulled a tendon. Peck was doubtful for Game 3, and perhaps the rest of the Series. It would be a huge loss for the Senators. His replacement, Ralph Miller, was nowhere near the player Peckinpaugh was.

In losing Game 2, the Giants seemed dazed. They had figured that if they could beat Walter Johnson, the rest of the Washington pitchers would be a piece of cake. They hadn't counted on Tom Zachary pitching such a great game.

Afterwards, Senators manager Bucky Harris held court. "We are just as good as they are," he told the press. "We found our true form today. We've got the punch to win, and everything that the Giants did to beat us yesterday we turned around and did today."

Both teams rushed to change clothes and get to the train station. The next three games would be played in New York.

GAME 3. Four days earlier a schoolteacher named Joseph Folby left his home in Springfield, Illinois. He got in his car and set out for New York City. Folby was the first person in line at the Polo Grounds when the gates opened at ten o'clock. Behind him, 50,000 others waited. Half of them, it seemed, were rooting for the Washington Senators.

The fans in New York were noisier and less dignified than the Washington crowd. The only politician in attendance was New York Mayor Hylan, and he excused himself after the second inning by saying, "I have a $375,000 budget to take care of."

In place of government officials were celebrities— heavyweight champion Jack Dempsey, entertainers Al Jolson and Will Rogers. From the baseball world, Casey Stengel, Christy Mathewson, and Rogers Hornsby were spotted in the crowd.

Down in Washington, fans could still see the World Series—sort of. At Griffith Stadium, hundreds paid to watch a group of United States Marines carry out a pantomime of the game based on the radio play-by-play.

Just before game time, two huge flower displays were delivered to the managers. Bucky Harris gladly accepted his in front of the Washington dugout. John McGraw, who was a very superstitious man, wanted no part of the flowers. "That's the surest jinx in baseball," he explained.

Hugh McQuillan (14–8) was the starter for the Giants; Fred Marberry (11–12, with 15 saves) for the Senators. Marberry was called Firpo because he looked like boxer Luis Firpo.

Both pitchers made it through the first inning, but that was about it. Neither was still in the game by the fifth. Eight pitchers would see work that afternoon.

The Giants got things started in the second inning when Bill Terry singled to right on the first pitch. Travis Jackson hit a grounder to third that had double play written all over it, but Ossie Bluege botched it and everybody was safe. The Giants scored when Hank Gowdy singled to left, and they tallied another run on a wild pitch by Marberry. They added a third run the next inning on two singles and a double play.

Giants 3, Senators 0. Firpo Marberry clearly didn't have his best stuff. In the first three innings, he gave up five hits, two walks, and a wild pitch, and he hit a batter.

But it wasn't Hugh McQuillan's day either. In the fourth inning, he walked Senators leadoff hitter Sam Rice. Goose Goslin hit a pop fly to short center that Frank Frisch snared in a desperate, running, back-to-home-plate catch. Joe Judge slammed a double to leftfield, putting runners at second and third. McQuillan walked Ossie Bluege on a full count to load the bases.

Ralph Miller, the replacement for the injured Roger Peckinpaugh, was up. He hit a sacrifice fly to centerfield and the Senators were on the scoreboard. Two walks brought in another run and it was Giants 3, Senators 2.

Two relief pitchers came in the game, Allen Russell for Washington and Rosy Ryan for New York. In the bottom of the fourth inning, Ryan got a rare turn to hit and surprised everyone by ramming Russell's 2–1 fastball into the upper deck of the rightfield stands. It was the first homer in Ryan's career, and the first *ever* by a National League pitcher in a World Series. Giants 4, Senators 2.

The Giants made it 5–2 in the sixth inning on a double by Fred Lindstrom. Each team picked up a run in the eighth, and the Senators were still three runs behind going into the ninth.

Bucky Harris started the Senators' final inning with a pop over the infield. Kelly, Wilson, and Jackson all tried for it, but the ball fell between them. Sam Rice popped up for the first out, but Goose Goslin beat out a bunt. Runners at first and second. Joe Judge represented the tying run at the plate.

Judge had already made two hits in the game, and he calmly stroked a single to right. The bases were loaded with one out. Now the tying run was at first and the winning run at the plate.

That was all for Rosy Ryan. Claude Jonnard came in to replace him.

But Jonnard couldn't find the plate. He walked Ossie Bluege to force in a run. Giants 6, Senators 4.

The bases were *still* loaded and now the tying run was at second and the winning run at first. A single would tie it. An extra base hit could win the game for the Senators. With one out, they had two chances to get those runs home.

"The bases were full and 50,000 were shouting like madmen," reported *The New York Times*.

John McGraw quickly yanked Jonnard before he could do any more damage. Mule Watson, a tall right-hander, strolled in from the Giants bullpen as if he were taking his dog for a walk. Watson seemed oblivious to the fact that this would be the highlight of his career, if not his entire life.

At second base, Frank Frisch yelled for Watson to hurry up. Mule broke into a trot the last few yards to the mound.

Ralph Miller stepped up to the plate. Everyone in the ballpark was thinking about Roger Peckinpaugh. If Peck hadn't hurt himself on his game-winning hit the day before, *he* would be in the batter's box instead of Miller. And Peck was a far better hitter.

Washington fans' hopes were crushed when Miller fouled out. Two outs. Muddy Ruel, the last hope for Washington, grounded to third to end the game.

Final score: Giants 6, Senators 4. The Giants were now leading the World Series two games to one.

Mule Watson strolled off the mound as casually as he had strolled on. But his back and shoulders were red from the slaps of congratulations he received from his teammates.

"This club isn't beaten yet by a long way," said the frustrated Bucky Harris. "Tomorrow is another game."

Maybe Bucky should have refused those flowers.

GAME 4. There were no baseball card shows in 1924. Ballplayers considered signing autographs to be part of their job. Before Game 4, Walter Johnson stood near the fence and signed any scrap of paper fans thrust at him. One reporter counted that Johnson signed his name 66 times in 20 minutes.

During batting practice, a few Washington rooters approached Senators owner Clark Griffith in his private box. "How does it look for the boys today?" piped up one fan.

"They can't lick us, pal," Griffith replied.

As Goose Goslin took his swings in the batting cage, Babe Ruth walked over. Ruth noticed that Goose had changed his batting stance slightly. Goslin had hit a homer in the Series, but only had three hits in 15 at-bats.

Goslin thanked the Sultan of Swat for the tip and made a mental note to correct his stance during the game.

The starting pitchers for Game 4 were Virgil Barnes (16–10) for the Giants and lefthander George Mogridge (16–11) for the Senators. Tall and thin, Mogridge had injured his pitching elbow a month earlier. John McGraw ordered his hitters to take one called strike from Mogridge before swinging at a pitch. McGraw believed Mogridge would tire more quickly that way, and then the Giants could go on the attack.

It looked like Mogridge was tired right from the start of the game. In the first inning, the Giants scored a cheap run on a walk, a ground out, and an error. Giants 1, Senators 0.

But actually, George Mogridge just needed to get warmed up. He settled down after the first inning. While the Giants stood at the plate waiting for the first strike, Mogridge gladly supplied it. He buzzed the first pitch right down the middle for just about every batter. That put him ahead in the count, and put the Giants hitters at a disadvantage. Inning after inning, a zero appeared on the Giants half of the scoreboard.

It was New York pitcher Virgil Barnes who was tired. In the third inning, he gave up singles to Earl McNeely and Bucky Harris. That brought up Goose Goslin. Remembering what Babe Ruth had told him before the game, Goslin changed his batting stance. The first pitch to him was a low curveball, and he golfed it all the way into the rightfield stands. Suddenly the Senators were ahead 3–1.

Two innings later, McNeely and Harris singled again. This time Goslin rapped a single to left, and it was Senators 5, Giants 1.

Goslin led off the eighth inning with *another* single, his fourth hit of the game. What Babe Ruth told him certainly seemed to be working. Goose came around to score on singles by Joe Judge and Ossie Bluege. By the time the Senators rally was over, they were leading by the score of 7–2. The game was becoming a rout.

But not so fast! After pitching a three-hitter through seven innings, George Mogridge finally did tire. In the eighth, he walked Pep Youngs and Irish Meusel on eight pitches. When Mogridge threw two balls to Hack Wilson, manager Bucky Harris realized his pitcher was exhausted and quickly called in Firpo Marberry from the Washington bullpen.

The new pitcher didn't bother Hack Wilson. He slammed the ball off the rightfield wall. Pep Youngs scored easily, making it a 7–3 game. Meusel tried to score, too, but the Senators got the ball in quickly and he was out at home plate by a foot.

The Giants scored another run in the ninth inning to make it 7–4. They managed to get two runners on base after that, with one out. A homer would tie it up. But Firpo Marberry got Pep Youngs on a grounder to first and punched out George Kelly on three pitches to end the game.

Final score: Senators 7, Giants 4. Once more, the World Series was even. The Giants and Senators had each won two games.

"We lost a pretty good ballgame today," commented John McGraw afterwards. "But we'll get 'em. Have no fear."

Giants catcher Hank Gowdy told reporters, "We're not licked by a long shot."

During the sixth inning of this game, the crowd cheered as Walter Johnson trotted out to the Washington bullpen. Some fans thought Johnson would be coming in as a relief pitcher, but the Big Train was just loosening up his long right arm. He would be starting Game 5, perhaps his last chance to win a World Series game.

GAME 5. The Giants scratched out a run in the third inning off Walter Johnson on two infield hits and a clean single by pitcher Jack Bentley. The Senators came right back the next inning and tied it with two singles and a bunt. Giants 1, Senators 1.

From the start, Walter Johnson didn't look like the Walter Johnson of old. His fastball wasn't all that fast. He wasn't striking out that many hitters. Maybe the strain of 18 seasons and a tough pennant race had worn down that famous right arm. The Big Train was running slightly behind schedule.

In the fifth inning, Giants catcher Hank Gowdy singled

off Johnson and Bentley struck another blow by clouting a homer into the rightfield upper deck. The ball was fair by two feet. Giants 3, Senators 1.

Bentley was also having a great game on the mound. In the sixth inning, he struck out the side. He didn't make a serious mistake until the eighth, when Goose Goslin (him again!) took him over the rightfield wall. It was Goslin's third homer of the World Series.

A shower of newspapers and programs poured out of the stands as Goose rounded the bases. The game had to be stopped twice while the garbage was collected. Giants 3, Senators 2.

Despite Walter Johnson's lackluster pitching, the Senators were only a run behind as the Giants came up for their turn in the eighth. But that's when things began falling apart for Washington. George Kelly led off with a sharp single to left. Johnson walked Bill Terry. Runners at first and second, no outs.

Hack Wilson got the sign to bunt, and he dropped one down the third-base line. Walter Johnson hurried over to pick the ball up, but it bounced off the heel of his glove. The bases were loaded with nobody out.

"Take him out! Take him out!" shouted some members of the crowd.

Bucky Harris walked to the mound from his second base position. He was nine years younger than Walter Johnson. He was Johnson's manager, but Harris also idolized the Big Train. In one of his first games in the majors, Harris had made an error that cost Johnson the victory. After the game, he was afraid to come into the clubhouse. But Johnson found him, put an arm around him, and said, "Don't worry about it, son. It happens to everybody."

If any other pitcher was in a situation like this one, Bucky Harris would have taken him out in a second. But Johnson might never get another chance to win a World Series game. Harris decided to leave him in and win or lose with the Big Train.

The New York Giants had no place in their hearts for sentiment. They had a one-run lead. The bases were loaded in the bottom of the eighth, nobody was out, and they had the chance to crack this game open.

Travis Jackson hit a fly ball to left that was deep enough to score a run, making it 4–2. Johnson got Hank Gowdy on a grounder to second, but the Giants still had runners at first and third.

Giants manager John McGraw decided to put on the hit-and-run play even though his pitcher Hugh McQuillan was up. McQuillan came through with a bloop single to left. That scored another run, and the Giants had a 5–2 lead.

Bucky Harris really should have brought in a reliever for Walter Johnson by this time, but he couldn't bring himself to take the Old Man out of the game.

Fred Lindstrom, who was exactly half Johnson's age, was up for the Giants. He'd already made three hits in the game, and he ripped a line single to left for his fourth. That drove in another run, and it was 6–2 in favor of New York.

When Johnson finally retired the side, he walked wearily off the mound, his shoulders drooping. The crowd stood and cheered, some of them screaming, "Win it for Walter!"

But the Senators went down weakly in the ninth, and Walter Johnson's dream of winning a World Series game appeared to be over. He had failed again, having been pounded for 13 hits while striking out only three batters. The Giants now had a 3–2 lead in the World Series, and they could wrap it up in Washington tomorrow.

"It's not very encouraging to know that I'll finish up my career in the big leagues with two World Series defeats," Walter Johnson said sadly after the game. "But I don't think I'll come back next year."

"It is better to have pitched and lost than to never have pitched at all," paraphrased *The New York Times*.

The Giants and Senators, escorted by a squad of motorcycle policemen, made their way to Penn Station. A special train was waiting to take them to Washington for Game 6. At Union Station in the nation's capital, 5,000 fans gathered to cheer Walter Johnson and the Senators—perhaps for the last time.

GAME 6. President Coolidge had other business to attend to, but Grace Coolidge persuaded him to put it aside and come to the ballpark. This, after all, could be the final game of the season.

The Senators weren't going to roll over and play dead—not if the baseball fans of Washington had anything to say about it. People brought cowbells, Klaxons, siren whistles, and even automobile horns to Griffith Stadium to make sure their rooting would be heard.

The noise began when Washington shortstop Roger Peckinpaugh limped out on the field. After his leg injury in Game 2, Peck had been riding the bench. But the World Series is something special, and Peck *had* to be out there with his teammates when they needed him most.

The starting pitchers were winners before the game began. Washington's Tom Zachary had beaten the Giants in Game 2. Art Nehf of the Giants had won Game 1. Nehf hadn't pitched since that game because a line drive had hit his pitching hand, causing it to swell.

When Nehf walked the first Washington batter on four pitches, the Giants bullpen started heating up. But Nehf regained his control and disposed of the Senators easily in the first four innings.

Tom Zachary was pitching well also, despite giving up a run in the first inning on a double by Frank Frisch and a single by George Kelly. Giants 1, Senators 0. Zachary breezed through the New York lineup after that. In the fifth inning, he retired the side with just three pitches.

The turning point of this game came in the bottom of the fifth. Roger Peckinpaugh hobbled to the plate to lead off for Washington, and he singled to left. Muddy Ruel bunted and Peck slid safely into second, sore leg and all. It was pitcher Tom Zachery's turn to hit. He tapped a roller to first. Peck struggled to third as Zachary was thrown out.

Runner on third. Two outs. The crowd was screaming for a hit so Washington could tie the game. Earl McNeely didn't get one, but he walked on four pitches and promptly stole second. Runners at second and third.

Bucky Harris was up. Nehf put two quick strikes past him, but threw the next three pitches off the plate. Full count. Harris rubbed his hands with dirt. He crowded the plate, almost hanging over it. He just wanted to meet the ball; hit a line drive somewhere to bring the tying and go-ahead runs home.

Nehf threw an inside curveball and Harris lashed at it. The ball shot to the right side of the infield, just out of reach of Frisch and Kelly.

Roger Peckinpaugh limped home with the tying run and Earl McNeely tore around from second and scored standing up. Senators 2, Giants 1. As usual when Washington scored, hats and canes and all kinds of objects were joyfully heaved from the stands.

Tom Zachary and Art Nehf kept rolling along, keeping the scoreboard clean in the sixth, seventh, and eighth innings. The Giants came up in the ninth, their last chance to pull out the game and claim the World Championship.

Tom Zachary was pitching a masterful game. He

hadn't walked a single batter, and hadn't allowed a Giant to reach second base since the third inning. Zachery got Pep Youngs on a pop out to third. One out. George Kelly singled to right, putting the tying run on base.

It was Irish Meusel's turn, and he slapped a hopper up the middle. Roger Peckinpaugh, his leg hurting like the devil, dashed over and grabbed it. Peck twisted around and tossed the ball to Bucky Harris for the force out at second. Then he crumpled to the ground.

There was dead silence in Griffith Stadium. The fans stood solemnly as Peck lay on the ground grasping his left leg. After a few minutes, he bravely tried to walk off the field, but it was no use. He was in too much pain. His teammates gathered around him and carried him into the Washington dugout.

One man started to applaud for Peckinpaugh but was stopped by the woman next to him. "This is no time to cheer," she admonished him. "This is the time to pray."

Meanwhile, the Giants still had the tying run on base with two outs. The dangerous Hack Wilson was up. Later in his career, Hack would have a spectacular season in which he hit 56 home runs.

But as a rookie, Hack Wilson was no match for Tom Zachary. Zach struck out Hack, and the ball game was over.

For the third time, the Senators had tied the World Series. Game 7 would be played on Friday in Washington. This would be the first World Series since

1912 that was decided by the margin of one game.

Washington fans, delirious with happiness, swarmed on the field. The Senators had to battle their way to the clubhouse.

The only Washington player who didn't join in the celebration was Roger Peckinpaugh. He was lying on a training table in a little room near the clubhouse, his head buried in a pillow and his leg packed with ice. Peck was finished for the season. But he had the satisfaction of knowing he made the play that saved Game 6, and he started the rally that won it.

In the Giants clubhouse, the saddest player was Pep Youngs. He had been counting on wrapping up the World Series and marrying his fiancée, Dorothy, on Friday. Instead of walking down the aisle, he would be chasing down fly balls in rightfield.

For six games, these two teams had swapped victories. The Giants won Games 1, 3, and 5. The Senators won Games 2, 4, and 6.

"We have been winning the odd games and seven is an odd number," said the superstitious John McGraw. "So if figures may be relied upon, we should win tomorrow."

Washington manager Bucky Harris disagreed. "This business of winning only every other game can't go on forever," he said. "I think it's going to stop tomorrow. We're ready to fight it out to the bitter end and that's what we are going to do."

GAME 7. John McGraw wasn't the only one who was superstitious. Three of the Giants—Frank Frisch, Pep Youngs, and Travis Jackson—wore bright red sweatshirts under their uniforms for good luck. Grace Coolidge wore her lucky necklace, from which seven ivory elephants dangled. The Senators displayed the flowers that McGraw had insisted were a jinx in front of Griffith Stadium.

It was a bright, sunny Washington day. Anticipation filled the ballpark. Even President Coolidge seemed excited. "On several occasions he actually shouted," marveled *The New York Times* in its description of the game.

The Giants and Senators lined up along the first and third baseline, forming an enormous V. As a group, the players saluted the president of the United States.

"May the best team win!" Coolidge bellowed.

This was it. Game 7. One of these teams would go home as World Champion, and the other would become a trivia question.

Giants manager John McGraw was known as a baseball genius, but it was Bucky Harris who set a complicated trap that would be the key to this game. Bill Terry had been *killing* the Senators in the Series, hitting .500. Harris wanted to get him out of the Giants lineup.

Terry only played when the Giants were facing right-handed pitchers. So Harris decided to start right-hander Curly Ogden and then *replace* him with a left-hander after the first batter. That would mess up McGraw's lineup, forcing him to pinch-hit for Terry and take him out of the game.

Curly Ogden was probably the Giants' worst pitcher. He had a 9–8 season, but a losing record over his career. He hadn't thrown a single pitch in the Series so far.

Ogden surprised everybody by striking out Fred Lindstrom on three pitches to start the game. He started walking off the mound, but Bucky Harris signaled him to go back. Seeing Ogden blow away Lindstrom, Harris figured he'd leave the right-hander in a while and see what he could do.

But Ogden walked the next batter, Frank Frisch. That was enough for Bucky Harris. He took Ogden out and brought in left-hander George Mogridge, the winner of Game 4. Mogridge retired the side.

John McGraw didn't fall for the trap right away. He decided to leave Bill Terry in the game even though Terry would have to hit against a left-hander. Terry grounded out in the second inning and struck out in the fourth.

The game was strangely quiet through the first three innings. The most exciting thing that happened was during the Giants half of the second, when a fan's cigarette ignited the tarpaulin near the stands. Firefighters rushed over and extinguished the blaze with a bucket of water.

The starter for the Giants was Virgil Barnes, the loser of Game 4. Barnes was looking sharp. Through the first three innings, he had a perfect game. He struck out four hitters, and the Senators couldn't get a ball past the Giants infield.

Barnes started the fourth inning by striking out Earl McNeely on a slow curve. But Bucky Harris rose to the occasion and slammed a pitch deep to left. Leftfielder Hack Wilson dove backward over the low wooden fence trying to make the catch, but the ball was over his head. It would have been an out in the Polo Grounds, but this was Griffith Stadium and it was a home run. Senators 1, Giants 0.

It was still 1–0 when the Giants came up in the sixth inning. Pep Youngs led off by walking. George Kelly worked the count to 3–1, then cracked a single to left. Giants runners were at first and third, with nobody out. It was Bill Terry's turn to hit against George Mogridge.

John McGraw knew this was his opportunity to stage a Giants rally. The game was getting late and he needed runs. Bill Terry didn't hit left-handers well, and McGraw didn't want to kill the rally with a strikeout or double play. McGraw decided to have Irish Meusel, a right-handed hitter, pinch-hit for the left-handed Terry. So Bill Terry was out of the game, just as Bucky Harris hoped.

Meusel stepped into the batter's box, and Harris set stage two of his trap. He took George Mogridge out and brought in Firpo Marberry, who was right-handed, to relieve him.

Meusel hit a fly ball to rightfield, and it was deep

enough for Pep Youngs to score after the catch. Giants 1, Senators 1. One out.

Hack Wilson didn't care if he was hitting against a lefty or a righty. He bounced a grounder over Marberry's head and into centerfield. Runners on first and third, one out. The Giants were rallying. The Senators and their fans grew apprehensive.

Travis Jackson was the next hitter. He slapped a playable grounder to first, but Joe Judge fumbled it. Kelly sprinted home and the Giants were ahead 2–1. Runners on first and second, one out.

Hank Gowdy was up, and he also hit an easy grounder. Washington shortstop Ossie Bluege could have ended the inning with a double play. Instead, the ball rolled right through his legs. Another run scored, and very quickly the Giants had jumped to a 3–1 lead.

Gloom descended over Griffith Stadium. Grace Coolidge wore a worried look on her face and nervously banged one hand against the other. It looked like Harris's plan had backfired on the Senators.

Few noticed that a tall right-hander had begun warming up in the Senators bullpen—Walter Johnson.

Giants pitcher Virgil Barnes was pitching the game of his life, a three-hitter through seven innings. When he got Ossie Bluege to foul out leading off the eighth, the crowd groaned. The end was nearing for Washington. Five more outs and the Giants would be World Champs.

Nemo Leibold was sent up to pinch hit for the Senators. Leibold got his nickname because he resembled the comic strip character Little Nemo. He took a rip at a Barnes fastball and hit a bullet down the third-base line. The ball grazed third base and went into leftfield for a double. The tying run was at the plate.

Muddy Ruel was up for Washington. He was the only regular player on either team who had yet to make a hit in the World Series. Maybe he was just waiting for the moment when he *needed* one. Ruel whacked a single off Kelly's glove at first base. Washington had runners at first and third. Hope filled the air for Senators fans once more.

It was Firpo Marberry's turn to hit, and rookie catcher Bennie Tate was sent up in his place. Barnes walked Tate with a full count to load the bases.

Washington had the tying run at second base, the go-ahead run at first. Earl McNeely was up. The crowd was screaming now. Mrs. Coolidge fondled the elephants on her lucky necklace.

With a 1–0 count, McNeely hit a fly ball to short left-field. Irish Meusel caught it for the second out. The three Washington runners held their bases.

That left it up to Bucky Harris, who already had two hits in the game. Barnes got two strikes past Harris. On the next pitch, Harris hit a hard grounder to third. It looked like a routine play, but the ball struck a pebble several feet in front of third baseman Fred Lindstrom. The ball rocketed upward and hopped a foot over his head into leftfield.

Ruel and Leibold dashed home madly. The Senators, miraculously, had tied the game. Giants 3, Senators 3.

Confetti flew off the upper deck, covering the field with what *The New York Times* called "a white mass that looked like the first snow of winter." President Coolidge became so excited that he dropped his cigar and applauded vigorously.

While the field was cleaned up, John McGraw replaced Virgil Barnes with Art Nehf. Nehf had been the losing pitcher the day before, but he retired the side and the game went into the ninth inning tied.

Having pinch hit for Firpo Marberry, Bucky Harris had to bring in a new pitcher, and the Washington relief staff was depleted. All eyes turned toward the Washington bullpen. The gate opened and a roar spread through the 31,667 fans in Griffith Stadium, like a fire igniting a stream of gasoline.

Of course! There was only one man to call in the ninth inning with the score tied and the World Series on the line. Walter Johnson walked slowly across the field, like a gunslinger coming down the street for his last shoot-out.

The crowd erupted with a standing ovation. Johnson had failed the people of Washington twice in the World Series already, but still they believed. This would be the Big Train's last chance to be the hero.

"You're the best we've got, Walter," Bucky Harris said as Johnson reached the mound. "We've got to win or lose with you."

Walter Johnson. Catchers were afraid to catch him. Hitters were terrified to face him. Even he was afraid of his own fastball—afraid he'd kill someone with it. (NBL)

Eighteen-year-old Fred Lindstrom must have been awed at the sight of Johnson, a living legend, coming in from the bullpen. He popped weakly to third, and probably was happy to get the bat on a ball at all. But Frank Frisch wasn't bothered by Johnson. He slammed a fastball to deep center for a triple.

The winning run was at third with one out. Some fans in the stands turned their heads away from the field. They couldn't bear to see the great Walter Johnson lose *again*.

Despite giving up the triple, Johnson felt his fastball was back. He intentionally walked Pep Youngs, then struck out George Kelly on three pitches. Two outs.

Bill Terry's left-handed bat might have done some damage against Johnson, but thanks to the trap set by Bucky Harris, Terry was out of the game. Irish Meusel was up. He rolled a harmless grounder to third to end the inning.

But the Senators had to score a run to win. In the bottom of the ninth they got a runner to third base with one out, but a double play wiped out the rally. One way or another, the World Series would end in extra innings.

Johnson walked Hack Wilson leading off the tenth. But he struck out Travis Jackson and induced Hank Gowdy to ground into a double play. His fastball was moving, and it was getting harder to see it as the sun dropped lower in the afternoon sky.

The Giants threatened again in the eleventh inning. Pinch hitter Heinie Groh led off with a single and Fred

Lindstrom bunted him over to second. But Walter Johnson didn't choke. He struck out Frank Frisch and George Kelly to end the inning.

It was a different Walter Johnson from the man who pitched Game 1 and Game 5. He was more desperate, but he was cooler. He was pitching on guts. This would be the final performance of his career, and he wanted to be remembered as the pitcher he once was.

In the top of the twelfth, Irish Meusel hit Johnson's first pitch to right for a single. But once again Johnson found a little extra in that old right arm. He fanned Hack Wilson and got Jackson and Gowdy on a grounder and a fly ball.

Johnson was getting into trouble every inning, but somehow managing to work his way out of it. He was pitching as if he was 25 years old again. The Big Train had struck out five Giants in four innings. But how much longer could he keep it up?

The Senators hitters weren't doing much against Giants relievers Hugh McQuillan and Jack Bentley either. The game was still tied at 3–3 as Washington came up for the bottom of the twelfth.

Ralph Miller, playing in place of Roger Peckinpaugh, grounded out to second. One out.

Muddy Ruel was up. He took a big cut, but got under the ball and hit a high pop directly behind the plate. Giants catcher Hank Gowdy hardly had to move. He

ripped off his mask, tossed it aside, and looked up to follow the path of the ball.

Gowdy drifted back about ten feet behind the plate,
and then forward again as the wind buffeted the ball.
Just as the ball began streaking down, Gowdy stepped on
his discarded catcher's mask. His foot became stuck, like
a bear in a trap. He tried to shake it loose, but he stumbled and fell. The ball dropped harmlessly a few feet
away in foul territory.

Muddy Ruel could hardly believe his good fortune. His
at-bat still alive, he banged a double down the leftfield
line. The crowd exploded. Washington had a runner in
scoring position who could win the World Series. And the
man stepping to the plate was none other than Walter
Johnson.

Johnson was a good-hitting pitcher. No, make that a
great hitting pitcher. He hit .283 during the season, and
one year he hit .433, the highest average ever for a
pitcher. During his career, Johnson slugged 24 home
runs. Now he had the chance to win the World Series
with his arm and his bat in the final game of his career.

Johnson didn't get a hit. He knocked a routine
grounder to short. But Giants shortstop Travis Jackson
fumbled the ball. Johnson streaked across first base
safely and Muddy Ruel stayed at second.

The crowd was on the edge of their seats. On the
mound, Jack Bentley was disgusted. If not for errors by
Gowdy and Jackson, he would have been out of the in-

ning. Instead, there were Senators on first and second with one out. Earl McNeely was up.

Everyone who attended this game remembered the next play for the rest of their lives.

McNeely chopped a grounder toward third. Third baseman Fred Lindstrom had two options: He could step on third and throw to first for an inning-ending double play, or he could throw to second to begin a "round-the-horn" double play.

But Lindstrom hadn't counted on a third, highly unlikely scenario. Remember when the ball hit a pebble and bounced over Lindstrom's head in the eighth inning? Well, lighting struck twice. McNeely's grounder *also* hit a pebble—perhaps the *same* pebble—and hopped over Lindstrom's head into leftfield.

Muddy Ruel tore around third and barreled home. Giants leftfielder Irish Meusel ran in and scooped up the ball, but he realized he had no play at home. As Muddy Ruel crossed the plate, Meusel sadly stuck the ball in his pocket.

The Washington Senators had won the World Series!

Fans swarmed on the field and surrounded Earl McNeely even before he reached first base. Policemen formed a barricade around the Washington players to prevent them from being mauled by exuberant fans.

The city of Washington, as you might expect, went crazy. *The New York Times* reported, "The streets are full of jostling, joy-crazed citizens blowing horns, manipulating rattlers, firing pistols and making a din that can be heard for miles. On the banks of the Potomac there is bedlam and madness tonight."

Thanks to a great team, an incredible will to win, and a little pebble, the World Championship had finally come to the nation's capital. Walter Johnson had finally realized his dream—he was the winning pitcher of Game 7.

An hour after the game, thousands of fans were still waiting for Johnson outside Griffith Stadium. "We want Walter!" they chanted. "We want Walter!"

"I don't know how I could have stood if I had been blamed for the loss of the championship," Johnson told reporters after the game. "But winning today makes everything all right. If I never pitch another ball game, I will have this one to remember, and I'll never forget it."

For Baseball Trivia Lovers . . .

♦ Walter Johnson changed his mind and decided to come back the next season. He went 20–7 and the Senators won the pennant again. This time they lost the Series to the Pittsburgh Pirates. Johnson pitched again the following season, and he didn't retire until his leg was shattered by a line drive during spring training in 1927.

♦ During his career, Walter Johnson led the league in strikeouts 12 times. He won 416 games, more than any pitcher in history except for Cy Young. His 113 shutouts are a record *nobody* has approached.

Johnson's career strikeout total of 3,508 wasn't matched for nearly 50 years. In 1983, Steve Carlton and Nolan Ryan topped it. It should be remembered that most of Johnson's career was in "the dead ball era," when hitters tried to hit singles and didn't strike out as frequently as they do in modern baseball.

♦ On George Washington's 204th birthday in 1936, Walter Johnson was invited to come out of retirement and attempt to duplicate Washington's legendary feat of tossing a silver dollar across the Rappahannock River in Virginia. On his second throw, the Big Train deposited the dollar on the opposite bank.

♦ Walter Johnson and Babe Ruth were two of the first five players inducted into the Baseball Hall of Fame when it opened in 1939 (the others were Ty Cobb, Christy Mathewson, and Honus Wagner).

In 1942, old timers Johnson and Ruth faced each other in an exhibition at Yankee Stadium. It was billed as the greatest pitcher versus the greatest hitter of all time. Johnson played along with the show, throwing creampuffs to the plate. Ruth slammed Johnson's third pitch into the seats.

Four years later, Walter Johnson passed away in Washington. A year and a half after that, the world lost Babe Ruth.

♦ John McGraw didn't know it at the time, but 1924 would be the last year he would manage in a World Series. History had repeated itself for McGraw. Just as in

1912, he lost the World Championship because of a series of freak plays in extra innings of the final game.

"They got the breaks, but breaks are part of every ball game," said John McGraw sadly. "Defeat is just something that must be taken in its stride. It's part of life."

♦ One year after McGraw retired in 1932, the Giants and Senators met *again* in the World Series. This time the Giants won.

♦ The 1924 World Series was the only one the Washington Senators ever won. In 1961 the Senators moved to Minnesota and became the Twins.

♦ In 1955, Douglass Wallop's book *The Year the Yankees Lost the Pennant* told the story of a Senators fan who sells his soul to the devil in order to lead the team to the World Series. *Damn Yankees*, based on the book, became a hit show (1955) and movie (1959).

♦ Four rookies who played in this World Series reached the Hall of Fame. Fred Lindstrom survived those pebbles and went on to hit over .300 seven times. Bill Terry hit .401 in 1930, becoming the last National League hitter to top .400. The same season, Hack Wilson hit 56 homers and drove in an astonishing 190 runs. Nobody ever had more RBIs in one season. And Travis Jackson, who made three costly errors and batted .074, went on to become one of the game's best shortstops. He would hit over .300 six times during his career.

♦ Washington pitcher Tom Zachary became most famous for being the answer to one of baseball's most frequently asked trivia questions: Which pitcher served up Babe Ruth's 60th homer in 1927?

♦ Calvin Coolidge was elected to a second term a month after the World Series. The Senators' World Series victory probably had something to do with it.

♦ The story is told that Coolidge spoke so little that somebody bet a woman she couldn't make him say three words. The lady walked up to the president and said, "Mr. President, someone bet that I couldn't make you say three words but I know I can."

The president's reply: "You lose."

♦ Grace Coolidge was known as "The First Lady of Baseball" long after her husband passed away in 1933. Mrs. Coolidge continued going to baseball games regularly, and made it to the World Series in 1949 and 1950. She once wrote to some friends, "I venture to say that not one of you cares a hoot about baseball but to me it is my very life." Grace Coolidge died in 1957.

♦ In the last year of his career, Firpo Marberry became an umpire. He had been playing for the Detroit Tigers earlier in the year, so he was never assigned to ump Tigers games.

♦ After managing the Senators to the pennant in 1925, Bucky "Boy Wonder" Harris didn't reach the World Series again until he was in his 50s. Harris became the manager of the Yankees in 1947, and led them to *another* of baseball's greatest World Series. To read about that one, all you have to do is turn the page.

BOX SCORES

Game 1
Saturday, October 4, At Washington

New York	AB.	R.	H.	RBI.	PO.	A.
Lindstrom, 3b	5	0	0	0	1	3
aBentley	0	0	0	0	0	0
bSouthworth, cf	0	1	0	0	1	1
Frisch, 2b-3b	5	0	2	0	3	3
Youngs, rf	6	0	2	1	2	0
Kelly, cf-2b	5	1	1	2	4	1
Terry, 1b	5	1	3	1	15	0
Wilson, lf	6	0	2	0	4	0
Jackson, ss	3	0	0	2	6	
Gowdy, c	3	1	0	4	1	
Nehf, p	5	1	3	0	0	2
Totals	43	4	14	4	36	17

Washington	AB.	R.	H.	RBI.	PO.	A.
McNeely, cf	5	1	1	0	4	0
Harris, 2b	6	0	2	1	3	3
Rice, rf	5	0	2	1	0	0
Goslin, lf	6	0	1	0	2	0
Judge, 1b	4	0	1	0	6	0
Bluege, 3b	5	1	1	0	2	2
Peckinpaugh, ss	5	0	2	1	4	4
Ruel, c	3	0	0	0	15	2
Johnson, p	4	0	0	0	0	1
cShirley	1	1	0	0	0	0
Totals	44	3	10	3	36	11

```
New York ...........010 100 000 002—4
Washington ........000 001 001 001—3
```

New York	IP.	H.	R.	ER.	BB.	SO.
Nehf (W)	12	10	3	2	5	3

Washington	IP.	H.	R.	ER.	BB.	SO.
Johnson (L)	12	14	4	3	6	12

Game 2
Sunday, October 5, At Washington

New York	AB.	R.	H.	RBI.	PO.	A.
Lindstrom, 3b	3	0	1	0	0	7
Frisch, 2b	3	1	1	0	2	2
Youngs, rf	4	0	1	0	0	0
Kelly, 1b	3	2	1	1	14	1
Meusel, lf	4	0	1	0	1	0
Wilson, cf	4	0	1	0	4	0
Jackson, ss	4	0	0	1	1	2
Gowdy, c	3	0	0	0	6	2
Bentley, p	3	0	0	0	1	2
Totals	31	3	6	2	25	16

Washington	AB.	R.	H.	RBI.	PO.	A.
McNeely, cf	4	0	0	0	0	0
Harris, 2b	3	1	1	1	3	5
Rice, rf	3	1	2	0	4	0
Goslin, lf	4	1	1	2	1	0
Judge, 1b	2	1	1	0	15	0
Bluege, 3b	3	0	0	0	0	5
Peckinpaugh, ss	4	0	1	1	2	6
Ruel, c	3	0	0	0	1	0
Zachary, p	2	0	0	0	1	2
Marberry, p	0	0	0	0	0	0
Totals	28	4	6	4	27	18

```
New York .........000 000 102—3
Washington .......200 010 001—4
One out when winning run scored.
```

New York	IP.	H.	R.	ER.	BB.	SO.
Bentley (L)	8⅓	6	4	4	4	6

Washington	IP.	H.	R.	ER.	BB.	SO.
Zachary (W)	8⅔	6	3	3	0	0
Marberry	⅓	0	0	0	0	1

Game 3
Monday, October 6, At New York

Washington	AB.	R.	H.	RBI.	PO.	A.
Leibold, cf	4	0	0	0	2	0
Harris, 2b	5	1	1	0	2	4
Rice, rf	3	1	1	0	1	0
Goslin, lf	5	0	0	0	3	1
Judge, 1b	5	1	3	0	5	0
Bluege, 3b-ss	3	1	1	0	2	5
Peckinpaugh, ss	1	0	0	0	0	0
Miller, 3b	2	0	1	1	2	7
Ruel, c	3	0	0	0	7	0
Marberry, p	1	0	0	0	0	1
aTate	0	0	0	0	0	0
Russell, p	0	0	0	0	0	1
bMcNeely	1	0	0	0	0	0
Martina, p	0	0	0	0	0	0
cShirley	1	0	1	0	0	0
Speece, p	0	0	0	0	0	2
Totals	34	4	9	2	24	11

New York	AB.	R.	H.	RBI.	PO.	A.
Lindstrom, 3b	4	0	1	1	3	1
Frisch, 3b	4	0	2	0	4	6
Youngs, rf	4	0	1	0	2	0
Kelly, cf	4	1	2	0	2	0
Southworth, cf	0	0	0	0	0	0
Terry, 1b	4	1	2	0	10	0
Wilson, lf	4	0	0	0	4	0
Jackson, ss	4	2	1	0	0	1
Gowdy, c	4	0	2	1	2	0
McQuillan, p	0	1	0	0	0	2
Ryan, p	2	1	1	2	0	0
Jonnard, p	0	0	0	0	0	0
Watson, p	0	0	0	0	0	0
Totals	34	6	12	4	27	10

```
Washington ......000 200 011—4
New York ........021 101 01x—6
```

Washington	IP.	H.	R.	ER.	BB.	SO.
Marberry (L)	3	5	3	1	2	4
Russell	3	4	2	1	0	0
Martina	1	0	0	0	0	1
Speece	1	3	1	1	0	0

New York	IP.	H.	R.	ER.	BB.	SO.
McQuillan (W)	3⅔	2	2	2	5	0
Ryan	4⅓	7	2	2	3	2
Jonnard	0*	0	0	0	1	0
Watson	⅔	0	0	0	0	0

Game 4
Tuesday, October 7, At New York

Washington	AB.	R.	H.	RBI.	PO.	A.
McNeely, cf	5	2	3	0	3	0
Harris, 2b	5	2	2	0	2	8
Rice, rf	5	0	0	0	1	1
Goslin, lf	4	2	4	3	3	0
Judge, 1b	4	1	1	0	11	1
Bluege, ss	4	0	3	2	2	3
Ruel, c	3	0	0	0	5	0
Miller, 3b	4	0	0	0	0	2
Mogridge, p	4	0	0	0	0	0
Marberry, p	0	0	0	0	0	0
Totals	38	7	13	6	27	15

New York	AB.	R.	H.	RBI.	PO.	A.
Lindstrom, 3b	4	1	3	1	1	2
Frisch, 2b	4	0	0	0	3	0
Youngs, rf	4	1	0	1	0	0
Kelly, 1b	5	1	1	0	11	1
Meusel, lf	2	0	0	0	2	0
Wilson, cf	4	0	1	2	3	0
Jackson, ss	4	1	1	1	0	3
Gowdy, c	4	0	0	0	0	1
Barnes, p	0	0	0	0	1	1
aTerry	1	0	0	0	0	0
Baldwin, p	0	0	0	0	0	0
bSouthworth	1	0	0	0	0	0
Dean, p	0	0	0	0	0	0
cBentley	1	0	0	0	0	0
Totals	34	4	6	4	27	11

```
Washington ......003 020 020—7
New York ........100 001 011—4
```

Washington	IP.	H.	R.	ER.	BB.	SO.
Mogridge (W)	7⅓	3	3	2	5	2
Marberry	1⅔	3	1	0	1	2

New York	IP.	H.	R.	ER.	BB.	SO.
Barnes (L)	5	9	5	5	0	3
Baldwin	2	1	0	0	3	0
Dean	2	3	2	0	0	2

BOX SCORES

Game 5

Wednesday, October 8, At New York

Washington	AB	R	H	RBI	PO	A
McNeely, cf	4	0	1	0	1	0
Harris, 2b	5	0	1	0	8	2
Rice, rf	4	0	0	0	1	2
Goslin, lf	4	1	2	1	1	0
Judge, 1b	4	1	3	0	3	2
Bluege, ss	2	0	0	0	6	2
Ruel, c	4	0	0	0	1	1
Miller, 3b	3	0	1	1	3	1
aLeibold	1	0	0	0	0	0
Johnson, p	3	0	1	0	1	2
bTate	0	0	0	0	0	0
cTaylor	0	0	0	0	0	0
Totals	33	2	9	2	24	13

New York	AB	R	H	RBI	PO	A
Lindstrom, 3b	5	0	4	2	1	1
Frisch, 2b	5	0	1	0	1	6
Youngs, rf	3	0	1	0	1	1
Kelly, cf	4	1	1	0	2	0
Terry, 1b	2	1	1	0	12	1
Wilson, lf	3	0	0	0	3	1
Jackson, ss	4	2	1	1	1	2
Gowdy, c	4	2	1	0	6	0
Bentley, p	3	1	2	2	0	1
McQuillan, p	1	0	1	1	0	0
Totals	33	6	13	6	27	13

Washington .... 0 0 0 1 0 0 0 1 0—2
New York .... 0 0 1 0 2 0 0 3 x—6

Washington	IP	H	R	ER	BB	SO
Johnson (L)	8	13	6	3	2	3

New York	IP	H	R	ER	BB	SO
Bentley (W)	7⅓	9	2	2	3	4
McQuillan	1⅔	0	0	0	1	1

Game 6

Thursday, October 9, At Washington

New York	AB	R	H	RBI	PO	A
Lindstrom, 3b	4	0	0	1	1	2
Frisch, 2b	4	0	2	0	1	2
Youngs, rf	4	0	1	0	1	0
Kelly, 1b	4	0	2	1	11	1
bSouthworth	0	0	0	0	0	0
Meusel, lf	4	0	0	0	1	0
Wilson, cf	4	0	2	0	1	0
Jackson, ss	3	0	0	0	3	2
Gowdy, c	3	0	1	0	5	1
Nehf, p	2	0	0	0	0	4
aSnyder	1	0	0	0	0	0
Rynn, p	0	0	0	0	0	0
Totals	33	1	7	1	24	12

Washington	AB	R	H	RBI	PO	A
McNeely, cf	2	1	0	1	0	0
Harris, 2b	4	0	1	2	4	5
Rice, rf	4	0	1	0	4	0
Goslin, lf	4	0	0	0	1	0
Judge, 1b	3	0	0	0	11	0
Bluege, 3b-ss	3	0	0	0	1	3
Peckinpaugh, ss	2	1	2	0	1	4
Taylor, 3b	0	0	0	0	0	0
Ruel, c	2	0	0	0	4	1
Zachary, p	3	0	0	0	0	0
Totals	27	2	4	2	27	13

New York .... 1 0 0 0 0 0 0 0 0—1
Washington .... 0 0 0 0 2 0 0 0 x—2

New York	IP	H	R	ER	BB	SO
Nehf (L)	7	4	2	2	4	4
Ryan	1	0	0	0	1	1

Washington	IP	H	R	ER	BB	SO
Zachary (W)	9	7	1	1	0	3

Game 7

Friday, October 10, At Washington

New York	AB	R	H	RBI	PO	A
Lindstrom, 3b	5	0	1	0	0	3
Frisch, 2b	5	0	2	0	3	4
Youngs, rf-lf	2	1	0	0	2	0
Kelly, cf-1b	6	1	1	0	8	1
Terry, 1b	2	0	0	0	6	1
aMeusel, lf-rf	3	0	1	1	1	0
Wilson, lf-cf	5	1	1	0	4	0
Jackson, ss	6	0	0	0	1	4
Gowdy, c	6	0	1	0	8	0
Barnes, p	4	0	0	0	1	2
Nehf, p	0	0	0	0	0	0
McQuillan, p	0	0	0	0	0	0
cDell	0	0	0	0	0	0
fSouthworth	0	0	0	0	0	0
Bentley, p	0	0	0	0	0	0
Totals	45	3	8	1	34	15

Washington	AB	R	H	RBI	PO	A
McNeely, cf	6	0	1	1	0	0
Harris, 2b	5	1	3	3	4	1
Rice, rf	5	0	0	2	0	0
Goslin, lf	4	0	2	0	3	0
Judge, 1b	4	0	1	0	11	1
Bluege, ss	5	0	0	1	1	7
Taylor, 3b	2	0	0	0	0	3
bLeibold	1	1	1	0	0	0
Miller, 3b	2	0	0	0	1	1
Ruel, c	5	2	2	0	13	0
Ogden, p	0	0	0	0	0	0
Mogridge, p	1	0	0	0	0	0
Marberry, p	1	0	0	0	1	0
cTate	0	0	0	0	0	0
dShirley	0	0	0	0	0	0
Johnson, p	2	0	0	0	0	1
Totals	44	4	10	4	36	14

New York .... 0 0 0 0 0 3 0 0 0 0 0—3
Washington .... 0 0 0 1 0 0 0 2 0 0 1—4
One out when winning run scored.

New York	IP	H	R	ER	BB	SO
Barnes	7⅓	6	3	3	1	6
Nehf	⅔	1	0	0	0	0
McQuillan	1⅓	0	0	0	0	1
Bentley (L)	1⅓	3	1	1	1	0

Washington	IP	H	R	ER	BB	SO
Ogden	⅓	0	0	0	1	1
Mogridge	4⅓*	4	2	1	1	3
Marberry	3	1	1	0	1	3
Johnson (W)	4	3	0	0	3	5

CHAPTER

3

1947

New York Yankees

vs.

Brooklyn Dodgers

The Subway Series

Yogi Berra was a rookie in 1947. In Game 3, he hit the first pinch-hit homer in World Series history. (George Brace)

YANKS WIN SERIES, | O'

AGE TAKING FINAL | L

FROM DODGERS, 5-2 | I

Chief Pitcher Hero as 11th | Cit

Title Goes to American | as

Leaguers Before 71,548

RECEIPTS HIT $2,137,549 | NE

Dodgers Beat Yanks, 9-8,
With Casey Stopping Rall

Routing Newsom in 6-Run Second, Brookl
Reduces World Series Deficit to 2-1—
DiMaggio and Berra Hit Home Runs

A lowly worm turned in Flat-
bush yesterday and in the process
kicked up such a terrific uproar

Hughie Casey rose as an imp
trable barrier for Bucky Ha
American League champions.

al Attenda
cord at 389
Resigns Club

By JOHN D
The Yankees h
er all, and as a
nx Bombers
re in a long-
eball champic
e.

they brought
es to a close
erday in aln
on as they d
in the seven
se by a scor
nd the ace t
ed down the
athering of 71
whom Buc
ted all summe
"Gentlemen,
he 30-year-old
rry Valley, P
nimitable rel
the breach in
Yanks had gr
e fourth innin
nto, Bobby B
able Tommy
er allowed Bur
rome up for a
$12,000,000 w
ed.

A Startling Resignation
his to the Yanks, most suc-
fu. baseball organization in a
ory, came another world's title,
eleventh since it bagged the
, in 1923, and the first under
aegis of Larry MacPhail who,
usly, chose this dramatic mo-
to announce his retirement
esident w

Pitcher Frank Shea (left) went the distance, and Joe DiMaggio (right)
hit the homer that won Game 5 for the Yankees. (NBL)

Yankees Defeat Dodgers, 2
For 3-to-2 Lead in Worl

With Frank Shea beating the Dodgers for th
the Yankees won the fifth game of the world se
Field yesterday, 2 to 1. As baseball's autumnal
back to Yankee Stadium today, the Bronx Bomber
lead and need one victory to clinch the championsh
only four hits, striking out Pinch-Hitter Cookie L
of Friday's game, to end the contest with the pote
on second base. The rookie pitcher also drove ir

DODG

BEAT

WITH

Lavage
in 2 R
Spoi

s, 10-3,
ies Lead
ith Brooklyn

*A*pril 15, 1947. Opening day of baseball season. Ebbets Field. It was cloudy and chilly, but 26,623 fans were happy to be there to witness the historic event.

After the Dodger leadoff batter Eddie Stanky flied out, a 28-year-old rookie first baseman strode to the plate for his first major league at-bat. He had a pigeon-toed walk that would soon become familiar to all baseball fans. He wore number 42 on his back. He dug his right foot into the outside line of the batter's box and pumped his bat back and forth. He took his front hand off the bat to dry it on his uniform. Boston Braves pitcher Johnny Sain looked in for the sign, and went into his windup.

The young man at the plate wasn't any different from any other big league player, except for one minor detail—his skin was dark.

His name was Jack Roosevelt Robinson.

Being a rookie in the majors is hard for anybody. But as the first black man in 60 years to play in the big leagues, Jackie Robinson had the toughest rookie season any player ever had to endure. People screamed vile, unprintable things at him from the dugouts and the stands. Scribbled death threats arrived in the mail every day, as well as threats to kidnap his wife and baby. Opposing pitchers threw at his head. Runners deliberately spiked him as they ran past first base. When the Dodgers were on the road, hotels refused to rent him a room.

Two teams, the Phillies and the Cardinals, threatened to boycott the ballpark if Jackie Robinson appeared on the field. Even Robinson's own teammates didn't fully accept him. Before the season, four of the Dodgers circulated a petition requesting that Robinson not be allowed to join the team. When it was obvious that Jackie was there to stay, one of the Dodgers requested to be traded to another team.

Jackie Robinson didn't do anything spectacular in the field that first day. He grounded to short his first time up and went hitless for the game.

But three days later, Robinson hit his first home run. He went on a 21-game hitting streak. He was a terror on the base paths, one time scoring from first on a *bunt*. Robinson would go on to hit .297 for the season and lead the National League in stolen bases. He won the Rookie of the Year Award. He led the Dodgers in home runs, runs, and games played. And to cap off the season, he led them to the National League pennant.

In Brooklyn, the Dodgers were affectionately known as the Bums. This would be their fourth World Series, and they had lost the first three. They didn't have much hitting, and they didn't have much pitching. But they were scrappers. Second baseman Eddie Stanky always seemed to walk (148 times one season!)—then Robinson would follow with a hit and create some havoc on the base paths. Shortstop Pee Wee Reese, rightfielder Dixie Walker, or centerfielder Pete Reiser would drive the runners home and the Dodgers would be off to the races.

Catcher Bruce Edwards and outfielder Carl Furillo had good years, both hitting .295. The weakest link on the Dodgers was the pitching staff, but relief ace Hugh Casey always seemed to come in and save the day.

The manager of the team was Burt Shotton, who came out of retirement to lead the Dodgers. Shotton was one of the few managers who didn't wear a baseball uniform. He guided the team from the dugout wearing his street clothes.

The Dodgers looked like a Little League team compared with the New York Yankees, champions of the American League. The Yankees were playing in their 15th World Series, and they had already won it ten times. Led by stars such as Joe DiMaggio (centerfield), Phil "Scooter" Rizzuto (shortstop), Tommy Henrich (right-field), and Yogi Berra (catcher), the Yanks won an astonishing 19 games in a row in July. They cruised to the pennant by 14 games. The team got solid seasons out of leftfielder Johnny Lindell (.275), first baseman George McQuinn (.304), third baseman Billy Johnson (.285) and second baseman George "Snuffy" Stirnweiss (.256).

The powerhouse Yankees led the league in home runs, triples, runs, batting average, and slugging average. Their pitchers had more strikeouts than any other American League team, and the lowest earned run average. In the bullpen, lefty Joe Page was spectacular, winning 14 games and saving 17 more.

The Yankee manager was Bucky Harris, the 27-year-old boy wonder who led the Washington Senators to the World Series in 1924. He hadn't won another Series in the 23 years since then. Now he was a veteran manager, and leading the Yankees for the first time.

Now it was the Bronx Bombers versus the Brooklyn Bums—a "Subway Series" since fans could take the New York City subway from one ballpark to the other. Hotels in the Big Apple were so crowded that guests were asked to double up. "Now I know why they call it a Subway Series," said one out-of-town fan, "because that's where I probably will have to sleep."

This would be the first World Series broadcast on television, and many American families bought their first TV set just to watch the games. One Brooklyn bar installed two sets in separate rooms—one for Yankee fans and the other for Dodger fans. Putting both groups in one room would have been like throwing a lighted match on a pool of gasoline.

GAME 1. It was a cool October day, with a cloudless sky. Yankee Stadium, decked out in red, white, and blue bunting, was stuffed to the rafters with 73,365 fans. Seven thousand people paid $4 just to stand. To keep the peace, 650 police patrolled the ballpark.

The Yankees lined up along the first-base line, the Dodgers along third. Metropolitan Opera star Helen Jepson sang the national anthem accompanied by Guy Lombardo and his orchestra. Years later, Jackie Robinson would say that standing there with his hand over his heart was the greatest thrill of his baseball career.

Politicians like to show their faces at the World Series, and this one saw former president Herbert Hoover in the stands, along with the governors of New York, Connecticut, Pennsylvania, Rhode Island, and New Jersey.

An ailing Babe Ruth was escorted to a seat in "The House That Ruth Built." So were baseball legends Ty Cobb, Rogers Hornsby, Tris Speaker, and 80-year-old Cy Young. Young had pitched (and won two games) in the first World Series 44 years earlier.

At 1:30 pm, New York Mayor William O'Dwyer threw out the first ball and pitcher Spec Shea took the mound for the Yankees. He was called Spec because he had a lot of freckles.

Shea had been discovered while pitching for a semi-pro team in Connecticut. The Yankees played an exhibition game against the team, and Shea shut them out. The following year, Shea was invited to spring training. He had a sensational rookie year, winning 14 games while losing just 5. He would be celebrating his 25th birthday in two days.

Shea looked at the target from his catcher, Yogi Berra. Berra was just 22 years old, playing in *his* rookie season.

Shea burned in the first pitch to Eddie Stanky and umpire Bill McGowan called it a strike. The 1947 World Series was under way.

Stanky swung at Shea's next pitch and flied to left for the first out. That brought up Jackie Robinson.

By this time, Robinson had proven himself to baseball and the world. There was little fuss made about his being the first black man to play in the World Series. Even so, Dodgers *and* Yankees fans erupted in appreciative cheers. Jackie worked the count full, then took ball four to become the first baserunner of the game.

Pete Reiser, playing centerfield for Brooklyn, was up. Robinson danced daringly off first. That was his trademark—distracting and intimidating the opposing pitcher in order to steal second, to force a wild pitch or a balk, or simply to upset him so he couldn't concentrate on the batter.

Yogi Berra had boasted that Robinson didn't steal a single base off him when they played in the minors. The Yankees catcher knew he would be tested in the World Series.

On the second pitch to Reiser, Robinson took off. Yogi's throw was in the dirt and Jackie was safe at second. The Dodgers fans in the crowd shrieked with joy.

Reiser tapped a bouncer to Spec Shea for the second out of the inning. But Dixie Walker swiped a loopy single into leftfield and the Dodgers were on the scoreboard. If there had been any question that Jackie Robinson would be the spark plug of the Dodgers, it was answered. Dodgers 1, Yanks 0.

After that jittery first inning, Shea settled down. He would walk Robinson again in the third inning, and that time Shea committed a balk trying to hold Jackie on base (his only balk all season). But the other Dodgers couldn't get to Shea, and the Yankee pitcher held them to that single run through five innings.

THE STARTING PITCHER for Brooklyn was 21-year-old Ralph Branca. He was having the best season of his career, winning 21 games while losing 12. Most ballplayers refused to wear the number 13 on their uniform because they thought it was unlucky. But Branca wore it proudly—he was one of 13 children.

Branca had a reputation for getting rattled when there were runners on base, but he didn't have to worry about it for the first four innings. Twelve Yankees came to the plate, and 12 Yankees sat back down in the dugout. Branca struck out five of them. Through four innings, he was pitching a perfect game.

Then came the fifth, the horrible fifth as far as the Dodgers were concerned. Joe DiMaggio started things off with a grounder between short and third. Pee Wee Reese dove for the ball and stopped it, but he couldn't make the throw to first. George McQuinn walked on four pitches, putting Yankees runners at first and second with no outs.

It was a bunting situation. Yankees third baseman Billy Johnson was up. The Dodgers infield inched in. Ralph Branca seemed uneasy.

Johnson didn't *have* to bunt. Branca's first pitch hit him on the ring finger of his left hand. Now the bases were loaded with nobody out. The Yankees wrecking machine was ready to switch into high gear.

Branca threw a high curveball to leftfielder Johnny Lindell, who clubbed it past third base for a double. DiMaggio and McQuinn scored and the Yankees were suddenly ahead 2–1. Yankees shortstop Phil Rizzuto walked to load the bases again. Suddenly, Ralph Branca couldn't get a Yankee out.

It was Spec Shea's turn to bat. He was a good hitter for a pitcher, but Yankees manager Bucky Harris decided to gamble by sending up a pinch hitter. He hated removing his starting pitcher so early in the game, but the Yankees could blow it wide open right now with a rally.

Utility infielder Bobby Brown, who led the American League in pinch hits, stepped up to the plate. After Ralph Branca threw two pitches off the plate, Dodgers manager Burt Shotton leaned over to pitching coach Clyde Sukeforth.

"Go get him, Sukey. He's aiming the ball," Shotton said. "Bring him back with you."

Hank Behrman came out of the bullpen to take over the pitching duties. It didn't help. Behrman threw two more balls, and Brown trotted to first, forcing in the third

Yankees run. The bases were still loaded with nobody out.

Behrman got Snuffy Stirnweiss on a force play, but Tommy Henrich slammed a fastball into leftfield, scoring Phil Rizzuto and Bobby Brown. Yankees 5, Dodgers 1. It was a typical Yankees explosion—quick, efficient, and devastating.

Joe Page, the Yankees premiere relief pitcher, entered the game in the sixth inning. The Dodgers scored a run off him on three singles, making the score 5–2. They got another in the seventh on the electrifying baserunning of Pee Wee Reese. The Dodgers shortstop singled to right and stole second. Then, on a wild pitch, Reese came all the way around to score while Yogi Berra frantically scrambled after the ball.

But it wasn't enough. In the seventh inning, Babe Ruth left the ballpark, confident his old team would hold their two run lead. They did. The Dodgers had outhit the Yankees, six hits to four. But the Yanks squeezed more runs out of their hits.

Final score: Yankees 5, Dodgers 3.

GAME 2. "I'm ready!" the little Dodgers left-hander Vic Lombardi said before the World Series, "I'm always ready."

But Lombardi's first pitch was slammed into rightfield for a single by Snuffy Stirnweiss. It was a sign of things to come. Game 2 was a Yankees massacre, the only blowout in this World Series. Baseballs were rocketing off the bats of the Bronx Bombers, and the way the Dodgers played the field, they might as well have left their gloves at home.

The Yankees scored at least one run in each of seven innings of this game. They had 15 hits, including three triples, and a home run by Tommy Henrich. Everybody in the Yankees lineup had a hit except for Yogi Berra. Snuffy Stirnweiss had three. Even Allie Reynolds, the Yankees pitcher, got two hits. The Dodgers used four pitchers, but none could stop the Yankees onslaught.

It wouldn't have been so bad if the Dodgers defense had held up. But they couldn't do anything right. In the third inning, centerfielder Pete Reiser staggered under a fly ball, turned the wrong way, and fell down. It went for a triple. In the seventh he let a single skip through his legs to the wall.

Leftfielder Gene Hermanski lost a fly ball in the sun. Eddie Stanky dropped an easy double-play toss at second base. Jackie Robinson tore in for a squeeze bunt and ran right past the ball. Dodgers hurlers made two wild pitches.

The only Dodger who looked good out there was short-stop Pee Wee Reese—not a single ball was hit in his direction all day.

Except for a homer by Dixie Walker, Yankees pitcher Allie Reynolds had no problem keeping the Dodgers bats quiet. Reynolds was one fourth Creek Indian. In fact, he played for the Cleveland Indians the previous season. He had won 19 games in his first season with the Yankees, and he went all the way in Game 2.

The final score: Yankees 10, Dodgers 3.

Humiliated, the Dodgers slinked off the field. Down two games to none, they seemed hopelessly out of it. Manager Burt Shotton tried to make the best of a bad situation. "The boys got some bad baseball out of their systems," he told reporters after the game. "Tomorrow we'll be at home and it'll be different."

But Yankees fans were thinking, "Sweep, sweep, sweep." The Yanks would have Bobo Newsom, who had won two games in the 1940 World Series, on the mound for Game 3. When asked what he would do against the Dodgers, he replied confidently, "Ol' Bobo will murder them."

GAME 3. Ebbets Field in Brooklyn only seated 36,000 fans, which was about half the capacity of Yankee Stadium. Naturally, tickets for World Series games played at Ebbets were like precious gems. Three days before Game 3, a man named Nat Kopel set up camp near the ticket office with a blanket, pillow, and provisions enough to last until tickets went on sale.

Even the ballplayers had a tough time getting in. When the Yankees little (five-foot-six-inch) shortstop Phil Rizzuto approached the gate, he couldn't convince the police he was really a baseball player.

"Go on, beat it," a guard told the Scooter. "You can't even play for a midget team."

Maybe the Dodgers were inspired playing before their home fans. Maybe they were desperate. Or maybe it was the mysterious balloon that floated out of the stands and hovered over Bobo Newsom's head in the first inning. Whatever it was, something was different. The Dodgers came out smoking, and old Bobo didn't make it through the second inning.

That inning started innocently enough. Dixie Walker hit a hopper to short that Rizzuto scooped up and pegged to first. One out. Bobo walked leftfielder Gene Hermanski. Bruce Edwards followed with a double off the left-field wall. Dodgers 1, Yanks 0.

Ebbets Field erupted. There may have been half as many fans as there were in Yankee Stadium, but they sounded twice as loud. And this was just the beginning.

Pee Wee Reese slapped a single to center, and Edwards scored the second Dodgers run. Third baseman Spider Jorgensen flied to center for out number two.

Dodgers pitcher Joe Hatten was up next, and he plunked a single to left. That put runners on first and second. The first pitch to Eddie Stanky was a passed ball that advanced the runners to second and third. Both of them scored when Stanky crushed a double off the right-field wall. Suddenly it was 4–0.

That was all for old Bobo. He trudged off the mound and was replaced by rookie Vic Raschi.

Jackie Robinson greeted Raschi with a single to right. Stanky stopped at third. It was Pete Reiser's turn to bat, but Reiser had injured an ankle sliding in Game 2, and it was swelling up on him. Carl Furillo was sent up to pinch hit. Furillo's nickname was Skoonj, which was short for *scungili*, which is Italian for "snail." Furillo whaled a double off the scoreboard. Stanky and Robinson scored.

Ebbets Field sounded like a pinball machine. The Dodgers band struck up "We Won't Get Home Until Morning." Brooklyn looked like a different team than the pathetic bunch who lost the first two games. Dodgers 6, Yanks 0.

While Yankees rightfielder Tommy Henrich was up in the third inning, he asked the umpire to inspect the baseball. Out of the stands boomed a Brooklynite voice shouting, "The ball is all right, ya bum ya!"

The Dodgers added another run in the third inning and two more in the fourth. Nine runs should be enough to win any game. But this was the Yankees, and Brooklyn would need every run they could get.

The Yanks started chipping back. They put together three singles in the third inning to score two runs. In the fourth they got two more. In the fifth they got two *more* when Joe DiMaggio cranked a homer into the leftfield stands. That made it 9–6 and Dodgers fans started getting restless. A three-run lead on the Yankees was like a tie game.

Ralph Branca came in for the Dodgers to put out the

fire in the sixth, but the Yankees tallied another run on a double by Tommy Henrich. That made it 9–7.

Yogi Berra had been hitless in the first two games, so Bucky Harris sat him down for Game 3. In the seventh inning, the Yankees had a situation for a left-handed pinch hitter. Yogi got the call. He hammered Branca's 1–1 pitch over the scoreboard in rightfield. Dodgers 9, Yankees 8. Berra's homer was the first pinch hit round tripper in World Series history.

If the Yankees were to come from six runs behind and win this game, it would be a devastating blow to Brooklyn. DiMaggio and Company would be up three games to none, and the Dodgers would be psychologically beaten.

To start the eighth, a very determined Hugh Casey marched out of the Brooklyn bullpen. He had saved 18 games during the season, leading the league in that department. The Dodgers desperately needed him to save one now.

Casey came through, slamming the door on the Yankees hitters in the eighth and ninth innings. After Phil Rizzuto flied out to left to end the game, Dodgers fans let go a collective sigh of relief.

"My arm aches all over," said Hugh Casey, "every inch of it."

Final score: Dodgers 9, Yankees 8. The Yankees still led the Series two games to one, but the Dodgers had shown they could win too.

GAME 4. Ebbets Field was one of those irregularly shaped ballparks where balls would ricochet off the out-field fence at crazy angles. Before the game, Yankees pitcher Joe Page was hitting fungoes off the 40-foot right-field wall so Tommy Henrich could get used to the odd bounces. Little did he know that one of those bounces would determine the outcome of this game.

The Dodgers gambled by starting Harry Taylor, a big rookie curveball specialist. Taylor had won ten games and lost only five during the season. But then he pulled a tendon in his pitching elbow and could only throw four innings since his injury.

Taylor would only pitch to four batters on this day, and he didn't get any of them out. Snuffy Stirnweiss hit the first pitch of the game for a single to left, and Tommy Henrich followed with a single up the middle. Yogi Berra hit a grounder that looked like a double play ball, but Pee Wee Reese dropped the peg from Jackie Robinson.

It was a first inning nightmare for the Dodgers—bases loaded, nobody out, and Joe DiMaggio swaggering up to the plate. In the Dodgers bullpen, Hal Gregg began warming up furiously.

Harry Taylor must have been quaking in his spikes, because he walked DiMaggio on four pitches, forcing the first run of the game.

Dodgers manager Burt Shotton didn't waste a second. He yanked Taylor and brought in Hal Gregg. The Yankees still had the bases loaded with nobody out, but Gregg shut them down with a pop up and a double play. Yanks 1, Dodgers 0. It could have been a lot worse for Brooklyn.

The Yankees got another run in the fourth inning on a triple by Bill Johnson and a double off the rightfield scoreboard by Johnny Lindell.

Meanwhile, Yankees pitcher Bill Bevens was giving the Dodgers fits. They had expected to tee off Bevens, a mediocre right-hander who only won 7 games all season while losing 13. But the Dodgers couldn't buy a hit.

After four innings, a few people in the stands had noticed that Bevens was working on a no-hitter. No-hit games are rare, of course, and there had never been one pitched during the World Series. If Bevens could do it, he would be making baseball history.

Although Bevens wasn't giving up any hits, he was issuing plenty of walks. Two in the first inning. One in the second. One in the third. Two in the fifth.

Those last two hurt him. Combined with a sacrifice bunt and a ground ball out, the Dodgers managed to squeak out a run without getting a hit. The score was 2–1, and Bevens rolled on, walking a batter here and striking one out there.

The Yankees defense played its heart out to save the no-hitter. Johnny Lindell made a great diving catch of a foul fly ball from Jackie Robinson. Two drives by Gene

Hermanski were snared at the wall. Bevens had his first 1–2–3 inning in the eighth inning. He went into the ninth on top 2–1, and with his no-hitter intact.

In the top of the ninth, the Yankees had an opportunity to score more runs and give Bevens some breathing room. Johnny Lindell and Snuffy Stirnweiss both singled with one out. Bevens bunted to advance the runners, and the Dodgers fumbled the ball so everybody was safe.

Bases loaded. Dodgers manager Burt Shotton decided to bring in old reliable Hugh Casey to pitch to Tommy Henrich. The infield was at double play depth.

Casey threw Henrich a low inside fastball and Henrich slammed a grounder back to the box. Casey scooped it on the first hop and fired home for one out. Dodgers catcher Bruce Edwards fired to Jackie Robinson at first to complete the double play. The Dodgers were out of the inning and coming up for their last licks in the bottom of the ninth. They were still hitless and behind in the game, 2–1.

Bevens walked to the mound and took a deep breath. Three more outs and he'd have the first no-hitter in World Series history. More important, the Yankees would be ahead in the Series three games to one. That would just about put the Dodgers away for good. A momentary hush fell over Ebbets Field.

The first Dodgers hitter, Bruce Edwards, hit a fly ball to deep left. Johnny Lindell ran back, leaped, and grabbed the ball at the wall. One out. Bevens's no-hitter was two outs away.

Bevens walked Carl Furillo for his ninth base on balls of the game. Rookie outfielder Al Gionfriddo was sent in to run for Furillo. The Dodgers needed speed on the base paths if they were going to score that tying run. Now if only they could get Gionfriddo to second. . . .

Spider Jorgensen was up next for the Dodgers. He popped a foul near first base and McQuinn squeezed it in his glove. Two outs. One more to go. Last chance for the Dodgers.

Hugh Casey, the Dodger pitcher, was due up. Manager Burt Shotton looked up and down the dugout for a left-handed pinch hitter. His eyes fell upon Pete Reiser.

Reiser had been sitting the game out. He told reporters that he sprained his ankle sliding into second the day before. But actually, he'd chipped a bone in his foot and could hardly walk. During the first three innings of the game, he sat in the clubhouse soaking his foot.

But Reiser was the Dodgers' best hitter and would be a tough out even if he was hitting with one leg.

"Ain't you going to volunteer to hit?" Shotton asked him. With that challenge, Reiser grabbed a bat and limped to the batter's box.

Seeing Reiser hobble out of the dugout caused the Brooklyn crowd to erupt in cheering so loud, it was barely possible to hear the public address announcer say, "Batting for Hugh Casey—Pete Reiser!"

Bevens got two balls and a strike on Reiser. At that point, Shotton flashed the steal sign to Gionfriddo at first. It was a daring move, because if Gionfriddo got thrown out, the game would be over.

On the next pitch, Gionfriddo broke for second. He stumbled, but the throw was high and he slid into the bag just ahead of Phil Rizzuto's tag.

The count was now 3–1 on Reiser. Bevens needed two more strikes for his no-hitter.

Yankees manager Bucky Harris thought it over, then flashed the sign to walk Reiser intentionally. This was another risky move. Baseball wisdom says you should *never* put the winning run on base. But Harris was afraid of Reiser's bat. He decided he'd rather have Bevens pitch to the next hitter, Eddie Stanky. And he knew the Dodgers had no more left-handed hitters on the bench.

After ball four, Reiser limped to first and was immediately replaced by a pinch runner, benchwarmer Eddie Miksis.

So here's the situation: The Yankees held a 2–1 lead in the bottom of the ninth. Two outs. Dodgers runners were on first and second, ready to run on anything. Bill Bevens needed just one more out for the win and the no-hitter.

The Brooklyn fans were screaming for a hit, just *one* hit so the Dodgers wouldn't suffer the humiliation of being the first team in history to be no-hit in the World Series. The crowd was on its feet.

Eddie Stanky started toward the plate to hit, but was called back. Out of the Dodgers dugout stepped Harry "Cookie" Lavagetto, swinging two bats. Lavagetto, 32, was a ten-year veteran whose career was winding down.

Bill Bevens uncorks the final, fatal pitch that ended Game 4. (NBL)

He only came to the plate 69 times during the season, making 18 hits (.261).

If he was going to make the last out of the game, Cookie was determined to go down swinging. He took a big cut at Bevens's first pitch but hit nothing but oxygen. The pitch was high and outside.

Bevens fired another one high in the strike zone, and this time Cookie made contact. The ball sailed on a line toward that crazy concrete wall in rightfield.

Next came what Tommy Henrich would describe as, "the worst five seconds of my life." This is what was going through Henrich's mind: He could go back and try to make a spectacular game-ending catch, but if he missed the ball, both runners would definitely score and the Dodgers would win the game. On the other hand, he could play the ball off the wall and hold the winning run at third. But if the ball turned out to be catchable, playing it cautiously would ruin Bevens's no-hitter.

Henrich decided to go for it.

He raced back. But as he did, he realized the ball was *not* catchable. It sailed over his head and slammed off the wall.

The no-hitter was gone, but that was the least concern. Two Dodger runners were tearing around the bases, and Gionfriddo and Miksis could fly. Henrich had to play the carom cleanly to keep the winning run from scoring. Before the game, remember, he had practiced caroms off the wall just for a situation like this.

The ball bounced off the wall and back to Henrich. But he was too close. The ball ticked off the heel of his glove. He raced after it, picked it up, and whipped it to relay man George McQuinn.

Gionfriddo had already scored the tying run, and Miksis was rounding third. He received the green light to try for home. McQuinn winged the ball home to Berra, but Miksis slid across the plate in a cloud of dust ahead of the throw.

The game, incredibly, was over. Dodgers 3, Yankees 2.

Silently, Bill Bevens walked off the field. He had come within two strikes of the first no-hitter in World Series history. With one pitch, he had lost the no-hitter and had become the game's losing pitcher.

Ebbets Field went crazy. Dodgers fans leaped over the fences and knocked down the security police to congratulate the hero of the day, Cookie Lavagetto. They ripped his uniform as his teammates carried him back to the dugout.

Strangers were hugging each other. Two fans said they'd never attend another game, because nothing could match the one they'd just seen. "Don't bother writing about it," one reporter said to another, "because nobody will believe you anyway."

"Did you hear what happened, honey?" Lavagetto shouted into the Dodger clubhouse telephone. Cookie's wife, Mary, who had given birth to a baby boy three weeks earlier, could only sob with joy. When reporters got a chance to interview Cookie, he told them, "That's the top thrill of my life, without a doubt. Nothing else can happen."

Twenty minutes after the game was over, the door to the Yankees clubhouse was still shut. When it opened, reporters found the players sitting in front of their lockers staring into space.

"I wasn't even thinking of the no-hitter," Bill Bevens eventually said. "I knew it was riding, but never mind about that. I'm trying to win. We lost. Those bases on balls sure kill you."

Hugh Casey, who had thrown just one pitch, was the winning pitcher. The World Series was all tied up at two games apiece. Game 5 would be in Brooklyn, and the underdog Brooklyn Dodgers were flying high.

As Brooklyn announcer Red Barber signed off the air, he said, "Well, I'll be a suck-egg mule!"

GAME 5. The excitement from the Dodgers' incredible come-from-behind victory was still in the air the next morning. *The Brooklyn Eagle* ran the headline, MORE MIRACLES TODAY. Gladys Gooding, the Ebbets Field organist, entertained the fans arriving for Game 5 with two songs dedicated to Cookie Lavagetto: "Lookie, Lookie, Lookie, Here Comes Cookie," and "I'm Just Wild About Harry."

Spec Shea, the winner of Game 1, was on the mound

for the Yanks again. The Dodgers went with 22-year-old Rex Barney, who hadn't started a game since the Fourth of July.

Barney was one of the fastest pitchers in baseball, but it was well known that he couldn't hit the side of a barn. True to form, he walked two of the first three batters to face him. The Yankees loaded the bases with nobody out, just as they had in Game 4.

But instead of walking Joe DiMaggio to force in a run, Barney struck Joltin' Joe out. Miraculously, he got out of the jam without giving up a run. It looked like it was going to be another one of those games.

Barney held the Yankees scoreless through three innings, but he was walking batters left and right. After the fifth base on balls, Dodger pitching coach Clyde Sukeforth came to the mound. "Stop aiming the ball!" he shouted at Barney.

But Barney walked two more in the fourth inning, and that time he paid for them. The opposing pitcher, Spec Shea, ripped a single to left to drive in a run. Yanks 1, Dodgers 0.

Joe DiMaggio came up with one out and the bases empty in the fifth. He had been having a miserable day, hitting into a double play in one at-bat and striking out with the bases loaded in another. Barney was getting him on low fastballs.

With a full count, Barney threw another fastball, but

this one sailed about letter high. DiMaggio ripped it into the upper leftfield stands for his second homer of the Series and fifth in World Series play. Yanks 2, Dodgers 0.

Meanwhile, Spec Shea was pitching a gem. The Dodgers could only push across one run in the sixth on a single by Jackie Robinson. Yanks 2, Dodgers 1.

By the ninth inning, Shea was exhausted. He had hit a double the inning before (his second hit of the game) and the dash to third on a passed ball had left him ragged. Joe Page got warm in the Yankees bullpen.

Bruce Edwards led off the bottom of the ninth with a single. Carl Furillo bunted to advance Edwards to second. One out. The Dodgers had the tying run in scoring position. Shea got Spider Jorgensen to fly out deep to right for the second out of the inning.

The Dodgers were down to their last out, and it was pitcher Hugh Casey's turn to hit. Just like yesterday.

Out of the Dodger dugout stepped—who else?—Cookie Lavagetto. Cookie, everyone in the ballpark remembered, was yesterday's hero when he ruined Bill Bevens's no-hitter with a two-out double in the bottom of the ninth.

Today, it was the exact same situation: two outs in the bottom of the ninth, Yankees leading 2–1, with Lavagetto up, and the tying run at second. Could lightning strike twice for the Dodgers?

In the Dodger clubhouse, Al Gionfriddo was listening to the game in the "radio room." A reporter was in there writing down the plays in his scorebook. Gionfriddo said to him, "Go on, put down a home run for Cookie. He's gonna get it."

Shea was more careful with Lavagetto than Bevens had been the day before. He and Cookie dueled until the count was three balls and two strikes.

Full count. Bottom of the ninth. One-run game. Runner on second. It was now or never.

Shea served up a belt-high fastball and Lavagetto went after it.

Strike three!

The game was over. Yanks 2, Dodgers 1.

This time it wasn't Cookie Lavagetto who got mobbed by his teammates. It was Spec Shea. He did a little jig on the mound before the Yankees carried him into the clubhouse, where they grabbed him, pummeled him, and mussed up his hair the way boys do to show they're happy. Shea had pitched a four-hitter for his second victory of the World Series, and this time he went all the way.

"I wanted to square what they did to Bev yesterday," Shea told reporters after the game. "That hurt me almost as much as it did him. Boy, that revenge was sweet!"

The Yankees needed just one more game to win the World Series, and they were heading back to Yankee Stadium where Game 2 winner Allie Reynolds would be on the mound.

"We have said our baseball farewell to Brooklyn for

1947," said Tommy Henrich. "Now we'll try to give them something to remember in the Bronx tomorrow."

The Dodgers had lost a close one, but they weren't giving up yet. "We'll beat that Reynolds tomorrow," said pitcher Hugh Casey. "You can bet your life on that."

GAME 6. It was a beautiful Sunday afternoon. Yankee Stadium was jammed with 74,000 fans to watch Allie Reynolds duke it out with Dodgers pitcher Vic Lombardi. But this would turn out to be a wild one, and neither starting pitcher would make it through the third inning. In fact ten pitchers would see work in this seesaw battle.

The night before, Yankees leftfielder Johnny Lindell couldn't sleep. After breaking up a double play in Game 5, he felt a sharp pain in his side. Lindell went to his doctor in the morning, and X rays revealed a fractured rib.

He was having a great Series at the plate (7 for 16) and didn't want it to end. So he wrapped tape around his chest and didn't tell anyone about the fracture, even though he was in excruciating pain every time he inhaled.

For the third game in a row, the first three batters got on base. Only this time, they were Dodgers. Eddie Stanky, Pee Wee Reese, and Jackie Robinson each singled, loading the bases. Brooklyn would get no more hits, but two runs scored on a passed ball and a double play. On that play, Robinson barreled into Phil Rizzuto so hard

Jackie Robinson slides hard into Phil Rizzuto, upending the Yankee shortstop. Rizzuto still got off his throw to complete the double play. (UPI/Bettmann)

that the little shortstop took five minutes to get on his feet. Dodgers 2, Yanks 0.

In the bottom of the first Johnny Lindell hit a single, fractured rib and all. But the Yankees didn't score.

In the third inning Brooklyn got two more runs on doubles by Reese, Robinson, and Dixie Walker. The Dodgers led 4–0, and that sent Allie Reynolds to the showers. It looked like the Bums might run away with it.

But the Yankees roared right back. In the bottom of the third, back-up catcher Sherm Lollar led off with a double in the leftfield corner. That was followed by a wild pitch, an error, and singles by Henrich, Lindell, and DiMaggio. When all was said and done, the Yankees had tied the game at 4–4.

After his second base hit, Lindell couldn't stand the pain in his side anymore and left the game. He had made 9 hits in 18 at-bats (.500), but he was finished for the World Series.

The Yankees jumped into the lead in the fourth on singles by Aaron Robinson, Henrich, and Berra. Yanks 5, Dodgers 4.

The sixth inning would be the big one in this game. In the Brooklyn half, Bruce Edwards started things off with a single to right off Joe Page. Carl Furillo liked Page's first pitch, and he smacked a double in the leftfield corner. Runners on second and third. Cookie Lavagetto hit a sacrifice fly to right, scoring Edwards. Yanks 5, Dodgers 5.

Next, pinch hitter Bobby Bragan doubled to left to put the Dodgers up 6–5. After Eddie Stanky pounded a single to right, Page was out of the game. Bobo Newsom came in to pitch for the Yankees. Pee Wee Reese immediately smacked a single, his third hit of the day, and two more runs scored. Dodgers 8, Yanks 5.

To help protect the three-run lead, Dodgers manager Burt Shotton sent in the speedy Al Gionfriddo to take over leftfield in place of the slower Gene Hermanski. This would turn out to be one of the smartest moves a manager ever made.

In the bottom half of the inning, Brooklyn left-hander Joe Hatten retired the first two Yankees. But then he walked Snuffy Stirnweiss and gave up a single to Yogi Berra. Two on, two out. That brought the tying run to the plate, and its name was DiMaggio.

Joe's homer had won the previous game. A home run now would tie this game. Everyone in the ballpark knew DiMag could go longball at any time.

DiMaggio jumped on Hatten's first pitch and slashed a bullet in the direction of the low bullpen fence in left. The Yankees in the dugout stood up to watch the flight of the ball. A roar escaped from the crowd.

"Swung on, belted, it's a long one," shouted radio play-by-play announcer Red Barber. "Deep into left center . . ."

Little five-foot-six-inch Al Gionfriddo, who had just come into the game, began sprinting toward the bullpen. Gionfriddo had hit a meager .177 for the Dodgers during the season, and his career in baseball was shaky. He worked as a fireman during the off-season.

They didn't have cushy padded outfield walls in 1947. There were concrete walls and sharp fences. The ball was starting its descent and Gionfriddo could tell it was going to land near the low wire fence. A sign on the wall indicated it was 415 feet from home plate.

"Back goes Gionfriddo!" yelled Red Barber. "Back, back, back, back, back, back . . ."

The two Yankee baserunners had already reached home plate, and DiMaggio had slowed into his home-run trot.

Some call it the greatest catch ever made. Al Gionfriddo sprinted over, reached over the fence on a run, and robbed Joe DiMaggio of a three-run homer. (NBL)

Gionfriddo was running full speed. He waited until the last moment to peek over his shoulder as he got close to the fence. He saw that the ball was coming down over his opposite shoulder. He twisted around and stretched his glove out over the fence.

"He . . . makes a one-handed catch against the bull-pen!" screamed Red Barber. "Oh, doctor!"

Gionfriddo held his glove up with the baseball showing at the top of the webbing, like a snow cone. The crowd screamed. Even Yankees fans were roaring. They knew they had witnessed one of the most remarkable catches in baseball history.

DiMaggio was all the way to second base when Gion-friddo snared the ball. He kicked the dirt in frustration. When Joe took his position in centerfield after the catch, he walked around and around in circles. He couldn't believe the ball had been caught.

"The ball hit my glove," Gionfriddo would tell reporters after the game, "and a split second later I hit the gate."

The Yankees would load the bases in the seventh and put two runners on in the ninth, but Hugh Casey came out of the bullpen to make his fifth appearance in the Series and hold the lead.

Final score: Dodgers 8, Yanks 6.

After the game the triumphant Dodgers hugged and kissed their unlikely star, Al Gionfriddo.

"Kiss him again!" a photographer who had missed the shot shouted to Pee Wee Reese.

"Hey, let somebody else kiss the little guy," laughed Reese. "I'm tired of it."

Before the World Series began, nobody had given the Dodgers a chance to beat the mighty Yankees. But here they were, tied at three games each. It would come down—as the greatest World Series almost always do—to one final game.

GAME 7. Spec Shea had been the lucky charm for the Yankees, winning Games 1 and 5. Shea had just one day of rest and a blister on the middle finger of his pitching hand. But for the most important game of the season, manager Bucky Harris decided to roll the dice with him one more time. The starting pitcher for the Dodgers was Hal Gregg, who had relieved in Games 2 and 4.

The Dodgers came out punching. Eddie Stanky led off the game with a single. On the first pitch to Pee Wee Reese, Stanky took off for second. He was gunned down by Aaron Robinson, who had taken over the catching duties from Yogi Berra. (Yogi had not yet developed into the Hall of Fame catcher he would later become. To keep his bat in the lineup, Yogi was playing rightfield.)

Pee Wee Reese took a base on balls, and he tried to steal second, too. Once again, Aaron Robinson whipped a bullet to second to nail the runner. It could have been a big inning for the Dodgers, but the strong arm of the Yankees catcher wiped it out almost single-handedly.

In the second inning, the Dodgers used their bats

instead of their legs. With one out, Gene Hermanski ripped a drive to right. Yogi Berra tried to make the play, but the ball came off the low wall at a weird angle. By the time Berra threw the ball in, Hermanski was sliding headfirst into third base. He scored the first run of the game when Bruce Edwards singled to left. Dodgers 1, Yanks 0.

Carl Furillo followed with another single, and Yankees manager Bucky Harris immediately popped out of the dugout. Spec Shea would not be the hero today. Harris removed his star pitcher and brought in Bill Bevens, who had pitched the near no-hitter in Game 4.

Bevens wouldn't have to worry about the stress of a no-hitter on this day. The first batter he faced, Spider Jorgensen, slammed a shot to right that bounced into the stands for a ground rule double. Bruce Edwards scored, making it Dodgers 2, Yanks 0.

Carl Furillo would have scored on the play, too, if the ball hadn't bounced in the stands. Instead, he was thrown out at the plate on the next play—Hal Gregg hit a bouncer to short, which Phil Rizzuto scooped and threw home well ahead of Furillo's slide.

Even so, the Dodgers were battling. If they could keep up the pressure, Brooklyn would win its first World Championship.

The Yankees, of course, had a thing or two to say about that. In the bottom of the second inning, they began their comeback. Two Yankees walked, and Phil Rizzuto whacked a single off the third base bag to score a run. Dodgers 2, Yanks 1.

In the fourth inning, Rizzuto started things off with a single to left. Bobby Brown came up to pinch hit for Bill Bevens. On a 3–1 pitch, he doubled to left. Scooter scored, and the game was all tied up. Tommy Henrich singled to put the Yankees in front, 3–2.

All season long, whenever the Yankees got a lead they brought in Joe Page to protect it. The game was only in the fifth inning, but manager Bucky Harris decided the time was right. He called the bullpen on the telephone and asked for Page.

"He ain't got nothin'," bullpen coach John Schulte said.

"I don't care what he ain't got," barked Harris. "Send in Joe Page."

The Yankee Stadium crowd cheered as Page emerged from the bullpen in rightfield. The Dodgers had roughed him up the day before—four hits and four runs in just one inning. He was determined to make up for it. Throwing only fastballs, he began mowing down Dodgers one after another.

The Yankees added a run in the sixth. Phil Rizzuto was in the middle of it again with his specialty—a bunt single. It was his third hit of the day. Yankees 4, Dodgers 2. They picked up another run in the seventh on a sacrifice fly. Yankees 5, Dodgers 2.

The season was running down for Brooklyn. They had to get something going fast or it would be all over. But

Page was throwing bullets, and he wasn't giving up any walks.

The Dodgers went down in order in the fifth, sixth, seventh, and eighth. They couldn't hit a cheap single off Joe Page, who was throwing with renewed determination. Three more outs and the Yankees would be the Champions of the World.

Dixie Walker was the first Dodgers hitter in the ninth inning, and Page got him on a grounder to second. One out.

All-purpose utility man Eddie Miksis came up as a pinch hitter, and he managed to squirt a single through the middle. It was the first hit off Page. Runner on first, one out.

That brought up Bruce Edwards. He hit a sharp grounder, but directly at shortstop Phil Rizzuto. A perfect double play ball. Rizzuto played the grounder cleanly, flipping the ball to Snuffy Stirnweiss at second. Stirnweiss tapped the bag and threw to George McQuinn at first.

Double play! Game over. Series over.

This time there would be no unbelievable catches, improbable hits, or miracle finishes. After six wild games, the Yankees had whipped the Dodgers the old-fashioned way—methodically, with timely hitting, solid pitching, and airtight defense.

"That man Page!" exclaimed Joe DiMaggio after the game. "What a pitcher when the chips are down. Was he great!"

"I'm just about the happiest guy in the world," said Joe Page. "This makes up for everything, particularly that cuffing they gave me yesterday. They had their fun then. I had mine today."

For Baseball Trivia Lovers . . .

♦ Nine years after Bill Bevens came so close to pitching the first World Series no-hitter, another Yankee pulled off the feat. In Game 5 of the 1956 Series, Don Larsen pitched a perfect game.

♦ The three players who contributed the most memorable moments of this World Series never played in the majors again. Bill Bevens got a sore shoulder the next

Cookie Lavagetto (left) broke up Bill Bevens's (right) bid to toss the first World Series no-hitter. A few years later, they could laugh about it together. (AP/Wide World Photos)

year. Al Gionfriddo and Cookie Lavagetto were sent to the minors. Lavagetto's double that won Game 4 was his only hit in the entire Series, and the last hit of his career.

♦ This would be the last World Series attended by Babe Ruth. The Bambino died the following August.

♦ Two bench warmers in this World Series batted 1.000 and went on to bigger and better things. In the seventh inning of Game 6, the Yankees sent up rookie catcher Ralph Houk to pinch hit. It was his only at-bat in the Series, and he hit an infield single. Little did anyone realize that 14 years later Ralph Houk would be *managing* the Yankees in the World Series. Houk managed from 1961–1984 and won three straight pennants in his first three years.

The Yankees also used utility infielder Bobby Brown as a pinch hitter four times, and he came through with two doubles, a single, and a walk. Brown went to medical school in the off-season, and became a surgeon after his baseball career was finished. Later, Brown became the president of the American League, a position he still holds today. That's why every official American League baseball has the words *Bobby Brown* printed on it.

♦ After this rookie season, Yogi Berra developed into a great catcher and won the American League's Most Valuable Player award in 1951, 1954, and 1955.

During his 19-year career, Berra never led the league in a single category. But his team made it to the World

Series an incredible 14 times. Berra played in more World Series games (75), had more at-bats (259), more hits (71), and more doubles (10) than any player in baseball history. He ranks second in World Series runs (41) and RBIs (39), and third in home runs (12) and walks (32).

Yogi became most famous for his "Yogisms," strange wise sayings that he tossed off unintentionally mixed up. A few examples: "A nickel ain't worth a dime anymore." "You can see a lot by observing." "It ain't over till it's over." When Yogi was a child somebody asked him how he liked school. He replied, "Closed."

♦ Jackie Robinson's older brother Mack was a track star who finished second to Jesse Owens in the 200-meter race in the 1936 Olympics.

♦ The *second* black man to play in the majors in the twentieth century was Larry Doby, who in 1947 appeared briefly and hit .301 with 14 homers for the Cleveland Indians in 1948. Playing in the American League, Doby took much of the same abuse as Jackie Robinson did in the National League but received less glory.

♦ Jackie Robinson was one of *two* black players in the 1947 World Series. The other was Dan Bankhead, who came up toward the end of the season and became the first pitcher to break the color barrier. Bankhead appeared as a pinch runner in Game 6 and scored a run for the Dodgers. He would go on to a short career in which he won nine games and lost five. In his first major league at-bat, he hit a homer.

♦ The Dodger who had asked to be traded rather than play alongside a black man was Dixie Walker. At the end of the season, Walker changed his mind and said, "No other player on this club has done more to put the Dodgers up in the race than Robinson has."

Too late. After the season, the Dodgers traded Walker to the Pittsburgh Pirates for Preacher Roe and Billy Cox.

Dixie Walker came from a baseball family. His father, Ewart "Dixie" Walker, pitched for the Washington Senators from 1909–1912. Dixie's uncle Ernie played for the St. Louis Browns from 1913–1915. And his younger brother Harry played for the St. Louis Cardinals. Harry won the National League batting title in 1947, and Dixie won it in 1944.

♦ Jackie Robinson was *not* the first black man to play in the big leagues. There were many black players in the 1800s. The most famous were Moses "Fleet" Fleetwood Walker and his brother Welday. The color barrier went up in 1887, and no blacks were signed for the next 60 years.

♦ This was the Dodgers' fourth World Series loss. They lost to the Red Sox in 1916, the Indians in 1920, and the Yankees in 1941. The team would go on to win six pennants in the next ten years. In 1955 they won their first and only World Series, beating the Yankees four games to three. Two years later, they moved west and became the Los Angeles Dodgers.

♦ During the regular season, Jackie Robinson stole more

bases (29) than the entire New York Yankees team (27). Robinson stole home an amazing 19 times in his career, and once in the 1955 World Series.

◆ In 1941, many people thought Dodgers outfielder Pete Reiser could become the greatest player ever. He won the batting title as a rookie that season, hitting .343. But Reiser was reckless, and 11 times during his career he crashed into an outfield wall and had to be carried off the field. It was because of Reiser that warning tracks were put next to outfield fences in ballparks. Despite his many injuries, Reiser ended up with a respectable ten-year career in which he averaged .295.

◆ Pee Wee Reese quit his job as a telephone-company cable splicer to play professional baseball. He acquired his nickname not because of his height (five-foot-ten), but because he was a childhood marbles champion. A pee wee was a type of marble.

◆ Jackie Robinson was the first baseball player of *any* color to appear on a postage stamp. He also starred as himself in the movie *The Jackie Robinson Story.*

◆ A familiar sight at Ebbets Field was a sign beyond the fence that read, HIT SIGN, WIN SUIT. A Brooklyn merchant named Abe Stark awarded a suit to any player who hit a home run off his ad.

◆ Yankee pitcher Bobo Newsom was probably the most traded player in baseball history. He pitched for 17 teams in his 20 year major league career. The Washington Senators traded for him—and then traded him away—on five separate occasions. He played three times for the St. Louis Browns, twice for the Philadelphia Athletics, and twice for the Dodgers. Bobo won 20 or more games in three seasons, and lost 20 or more in three as well. He finished up with 211 career victories and 222 losses.

♦ Yankee shortstop Phil Rizzuto was one of the shortest players of his era. He was also one of the best, and he won the Most Valuable Player Award in 1950. The following season, the St. Louis Browns allowed a midget named Eddie Gaedel to bat in a game.

Midgets were quickly banned from baseball, and St. Louis owner Bill Veeck complained, "Let's establish what is a midget in fact. Is it three feet, six inches? Eddie's height? Is it four-feet-six? If it's five-feet-six, that's great. We can get rid of Rizzuto."

Phil Rizzuto was inducted into the Baseball Hall of Fame in 1994.

BOX SCORES

Game 1

Tuesday, September 30, At New York

Brooklyn	AB	R	H	RBI	PO	A
Stanky, 2b	4	0	1	0	0	4
Robinson, 1b	2	1	0	0	8	1
Reiser, cf-lf	4	1	1	0	3	0
Walker, rf	4	0	2	1	1	0
Hermanski, lf	2	0	0	0	2	0
bFurillo, cf	1	0	1	1	2	0
Edwards, c	4	0	0	0	8	0
Jorgensen, 3b	2	0	0	0	0	1
cLavagetto, 3b	2	0	0	0	0	0
Reese, ss	4	1	1	0	0	2
Branca, p	2	0	0	0	0	0
Behrman, p	0	0	0	0	0	1
dMiksis	1	0	0	0	0	0
Casey, p	0	0	0	0	0	0
Totals	32	3	6	2	24	9

New York	AB	R	H	RBI	PO	A
Stirnweiss, 2b	4	0	0	0	3	1
Henrich, rf	4	0	1	2	3	0
Berra, c	4	0	0	0	5	0
DiMaggio, cf	4	1	1	0	2	0
McQuinn, 1b	3	1	0	0	7	2
Johnson, 3b	3	1	0	0	1	2
Lindell, lf	3	0	1	2	3	0
Rizzuto, ss	2	1	1	0	1	3
Shea, p	1	0	0	0	1	2
aBrown	0	1	0	1	0	0
Page, p	1	0	0	0	1	2
Totals	28	5	4	5	27	12

```
Brooklyn ........ 1 0 0 0 0 1 1 0 0—3
New York ........ 0 0 0 0 5 0 0 0 x—5
```

Brooklyn	IP	H	R	ER	BB	SO
Branca (L)	4*	2	5	5	3	5
Behrman	2	1	0	0	0	0
Casey	2	1	0	0	0	1

New York	IP	H	R	ER	BB	SO
Shea (W)	5	2	1	1	2	3
Page	4	4	2	2		

Game 2

Wednesday, October 1, At New York

Brooklyn	AB	R	H	RBI	PO	A
Stanky, 2b	4	0	1	0	3	2
Robinson, 1b	4	0	2	1	5	0
Reiser, cf	4	0	1	0	4	0
Walker, rf	4	1	1	1	1	0
Hermanski, lf	3	1	0	0	3	0
Edwards, c	4	0	1	0	5	1
Reese, ss	3	1	2	0	0	0
Jorgensen, 3b	4	0	1	1	3	5
Lombardi, p	2	0	0	0	0	0
Gregg, p	0	0	0	0	0	2
aVaughan	1	0	0	0	0	0
Behrman, p	0	0	0	0	0	0
Barney, p	0	0	0	0	0	0
bGionfriddo	1	0	0	0	0	0
Totals	34	3	9	3	24	10

New York	AB	R	H	RBI	PO	A
Stirnweiss, 2b	4	2	3	1	1	2
Henrich, rf	4	1	2	1	3	0
Lindell, lf	4	1	2	2	2	0
DiMaggio, cf	4	0	1	0	4	0
McQuinn, 1b	5	1	2	1	6	1
Johnson, 3b	5	2	2	1	1	2
Rizzuto, ss	5	0	1	1	3	4
Berra, c	3	1	0	0	6	1
Reynolds, p	4	2	2	1	1	0
Totals	38	10	15	8	27	10

```
Brooklyn ........ 0 0 1 1 0 0 0 0 1—3
New York ........ 1 0 1 1 2 1 4 0 x—10
```

Brooklyn	IP	H	R	ER	BB	SO
Lombardi (L)	4*	9	5	5	1	3
Gregg	2	2	1	1	1	2
Behrman	⅓	3	4	4	1	0
Barney	1⅔	1	0	0	1	0

New York	IP	H	R	ER	BB	SO
Reynolds (W)	9	9	3	3	2	6

Game 3

Thursday, October 2, At Brooklyn

New York	AB	R	H	RBI	PO	A
Stirnweiss, 2b	5	0	2	1	2	3
Henrich, rf	4	0	1	1	0	0
Lindell, lf	4	1	2	1	0	0
DiMaggio, cf	4	1	2	3	3	0
McQuinn, 1b	4	0	0	0	8	1
Johnson, 3b	4	1	1	0	2	1
Rizzuto, ss	5	0	1	0	5	2
Lollar, c	3	2	2	1	2	1
eBerra, c	2	1	1	1	2	0
Newsom, p	0	0	0	0	0	1
Raschi, p	0	0	0	0	0	0
bClark	0	1	0	0	0	0
Drews, p	0	0	0	0	0	2
cPhillips	1	0	0	0	0	0
Chandler, p	0	0	0	0	0	0
dBrown	1	1	1	0	0	0
Page, p	1	0	0	0	0	0
Totals	38	8	13	8	24	11

Brooklyn	AB	R	H	RBI	PO	A
Stanky, 2b	4	2	1	2	4	5
Robinson, 1b	4	1	2	0	10	1
Reiser, cf	0	1	0	0	1	0
aFurillo, cf	3	1	2	2	0	0
Walker, rf	5	0	2	1	1	0
Hermanski, lf	3	2	1	1	4	0
Edwards, c	4	1	1	1	5	0
Reese, ss	3	1	1	1	1	3
Jorgensen, 3b	4	0	2	0	1	3
Hatten, p	2	1	1	0	0	0
Branca, p	1	0	0	0	0	0
Casey, p	0	0	0	0	1	1
Totals	34	9	13	9	27	13

```
New York ........ 0 0 2 2 2 1 1 0 0—8
Brooklyn ........ 0 6 1 2 0 0 0 0 x—9
```

New York	IP	H	R	ER	BB	SO
Newsom (L)	1⅓	5	5	5	2	0
Raschi	½	2	1	1	0	0
Drews	1	1	1	1	0	0
Chandler	2	2	2	2	3	1
Page	3	3	0	0	1	3

Brooklyn	IP	H	R	ER	BB	SO
Hatten	4⅓	8	6	6	3	3
Branca	2	4	2	2	2	1
Casey (W)	2⅔	1	0	0	1	1

Game 4

Friday, October 3, At Brooklyn

New York	AB	R	H	RBI	PO	A
Stirnweiss, 2b	4	1	2	0	2	1
Henrich, rf	5	0	1	0	2	0
Berra, c	4	0	0	0	6	1
DiMaggio, cf	2	0	0	0	2	0
McQuinn, 1b	4	0	1	0	7	0
Johnson, 3b	4	1	1	0	3	2
Lindell, lf	3	0	2	1	3	0
Rizzuto, ss	4	0	1	0	1	2
Bevens, p	3	0	0	0	0	1
Totals	33	2	8	2	26	7

Brooklyn	AB	R	H	RBI	PO	A
Stanky, 2b	1	0	0	0	2	3
eLavagetto	1	0	1	2	0	0
Reese, ss	4	0	0	1	3	5
Robinson, 1b	4	0	0	0	11	1
Walker, rf	2	0	0	0	0	0
Hermanski, lf	4	0	0	0	2	0
Edwards, c	4	0	0	0	7	1
Furillo, cf	3	0	0	0	2	0
bGionfriddo	0	1	0	0	0	0
Jorgensen, 3b	2	1	0	0	0	1
Taylor, p	0	0	0	0	0	0
Gregg, p	1	0	0	0	0	1
aVaughan	0	0	0	0	0	0
Behrman, p	0	0	0	0	0	0
Casey, p	0	0	0	0	0	0
cReiser	0	0	0	0	0	0
dMiksis	0	1	0	0	0	0
Totals	26	3	1	3	27	15

```
New York ........ 1 0 0 1 0 0 0 0 0—2
Brooklyn ........ 0 0 0 0 1 0 0 2—3
```

Two out when winning run scored.

New York	IP	H	R	ER	BB	SO
Bevens (L)	8⅔	1	3	3	10	5

Brooklyn	IP	H	R	ER	BB	SO
Taylor	0*	0	1	0	1	0
Gregg	7	4	1	1	3	5
Behrman	1⅓	2	1	1	0	0
Casey (W)	⅔	0	0	0	0	0

BOX SCORES

Game 5

Saturday, October 4, At Brooklyn

New York	AB.	R.	H.	RBI.	PO.	A.
Stirnweiss, 2b	3	0	0	0	3	4
Henrich, rf	4	0	2	0	1	0
Lindell, lf	2	0	0	0	3	0
DiMaggio, cf	4	1	1	1	3	0
McQuinn, 1b	4	0	0	0	7	0
Johnson, 3b	3	0	0	0	2	1
A. Robinson, c	3	1	0	0	7	0
Rizzuto, ss	2	0	0	0	1	1
Shea, p	4	0	2	1	0	1
Totals	29	2	5	2	27	7

Brooklyn	AB.	R.	H.	RBI.	PO.	A.
Stanky, 2b	3	0	0	0	2	2
cReiser	0	0	0	0	0	0
dMiksis, 2b	0	0	0	0	1	1
Reese, ss	2	0	0	0	2	3
J. Robinson, 1b	4	0	1	1	5	0
Walker, rf	4	0	0	0	0	0
Hermanski, lf	4	0	1	0	2	0
Edwards, c	3	0	1	0	9	2
eLombardi	0	0	0	0	0	0
Furillo, cf	3	0	0	0	2	0
Jorgensen, 3b	4	0	0	0	3	0
Barney, p	1	0	0	0	0	1
Hatten, p	0	0	0	0	0	0
aGionfriddo	0	1	0	0	0	0
Behrman, p	0	0	0	0	0	1
bVaughan	1	0	1	0	0	0
Casey, p	0	0	0	0	1	0
fLavagetto	1	0	0	0	0	0
Totals	30	1	4	1	27	10

```
New York ............... 0 0 0  1 1 0  0 0 0—2
Brooklyn ............... 0 0 0  0 0 1  0 0 0—1
```

New York	IP.	H.	R.	ER.	BB.	SO.
Shea (W)	9	4	1	1	5	7

Brooklyn	IP.	H.	R.	ER.	BB.	SO.
Barney (L)	4⅔	3	2	2	9	3
Hatten	1⅓	0	0	0	0	1
Behrman	1	0	0	0	1	2
Casey	2	1	0	0	0	1

Game 7

Monday, October 6, At New York

Brooklyn	AB.	R.	H.	RBI.	PO.	A.
Stanky, 2b	4	0	1	0	3	1
Reese, ss	3	0	0	0	0	1
J. Robinson, 1b	4	0	0	0	3	2
Walker, rf	3	0	0	0	1	0
Hermanski, lf	2	1	1	0	2	0
bMiksis, lf	2	0	1	0	2	0
Edwards, c	4	1	2	1	5	0
Furillo, cf	3	0	1	0	4	0
Jorgensen, 3b	2	0	1	1	0	1
dLavagetto, 3b	1	0	0	0	0	0
Gregg, p	2	0	0	0	1	0
Behrman, p	0	0	0	0	1	0
Hatten, p	0	0	0	0	0	0
Barney, p	0	0	0	0	0	0
eHodges	1	0	0	0	0	0
Casey, p	0	0	0	0	0	0
Totals	31	2	7	2	24	5

New York	AB.	R.	H.	RBI.	PO.	A.
Stirnweiss, 2b	2	0	0	0	5	4
Henrich, lf	5	0	1	1	2	0
Berra, rf	3	0	0	1	0	0
cClark, rf	1	0	1	1	2	0
DiMaggio, cf	3	0	0	0	3	0
McQuinn, 1b	2	1	0	0	7	0
Johnson, 3b	3	2	1	0	1	1
A. Robinson, c	3	0	0	1	4	2
Rizzuto, ss	4	2	3	1	2	2
Shea, p	0	0	0	0	0	0
Bevens, p	1	0	0	0	0	0
nBrown	1	0	1	1	0	0
Page, p	2	0	0	0	0	0
Totals	30	5	7	5	27	9

```
Brooklyn ............... 0 2 0  0 0 0  0 0 0—2
New York ............... 0 1 0  2 0 1  1 0 x—5
```

Brooklyn	IP.	H.	R.	ER.	BB.	SO.
Gregg (L)	3⅓	3	3	3	4	3
Behrman	1⅔	2	1	1	3	1
Hatten	½	1	0	0	1	0
Barney	½	0	0	0	0	0
Casey	2	1	1	1	0	0

New York	IP.	H.	R.	ER.	BB.	SO.
Shea	1⅓	4	2	2	1	0
Bevens	2⅔	2	0	0	1	2
Page (W)	5	1	0	0	0	1

Game 6

Sunday, October 5, At New York

Brooklyn	AB.	R.	H.	RBI.	PO.	A.
Stanky, 2b	5	2	2	0	4	2
Reese, ss	4	2	3	2	2	1
J. Robinson, 1b	5	1	2	1	7	1
Walker, rf	5	0	1	1	3	0
Hermanski, lf	1	0	0	0	0	0
bMiksis, lf	1	0	0	0	0	0
Gionfriddo, lf	2	0	0	0	1	0
Edwards, c	4	1	1	0	5	0
Furillo, cf	4	1	2	0	4	1
Jorgensen, 3b	2	0	0	0	1	1
cLavagetto, 3b	2	0	0	1	0	1
Lombardi, c	1	0	0	0	0	0
Branca, p	1	0	0	0	0	1
dBragan	1	0	1	1	0	0
eBankhead	0	1	0	0	0	0
Hatten, p	1	0	0	0	0	0
Casey, p	0	0	0	0	0	0
Totals	39	8	12	6	27	9

New York	AB.	R.	H.	RBI.	PO.	A.
Stirnweiss, 2b	5	0	1	1	1	6
Henrich, rf-lf	5	1	2	0	1	0
Lindell, lf	2	1	2	1	1	0
Berra, rf	3	0	2	1	1	0
DiMaggio, cf	5	1	1	0	5	0
Johnson, 3b	5	2	1	1	5	5
Phillips, 1b	1	0	0	0	4	0
aBrown	1	0	1	1	0	0
McQuinn, 1b	1	0	0	0	6	0
Rizzuto, ss	4	0	1	0	6	1
Lollar, c	1	1	1	0	0	0
A. Robinson, c	4	1	2	0	2	0
Reynolds, p	0	0	0	0	0	0
Drews, p	2	0	0	0	0	0
Page, p	0	0	0	0	0	0
Newsom, p	0	0	0	0	0	0
fClark	1	0	0	0	0	0
Raschi, p	0	0	0	0	0	0
gHouk	1	0	1	0	0	0
Wensloff, p	0	0	0	0	0	1
hFrey	1	0	0	0	0	0
Totals	42	6	15	6	27	14

```
Brooklyn ............... 2 0 2  0 0 4  0 0 0—8
New York ............... 0 0 4  1 0 0  0 0 1—6
```

Brooklyn	IP.	H.	R.	ER.	BB.	SO.
Lombardi	2⅔	5	4	4	0	2
Branca (W)	2⅓	6	1	1	0	2
Hatten	3⅔	3	1	1	4	0
Casey	1	1	0	0	0	0

New York	IP.	H.	R.	ER.	BB.	SO.
Reynolds	2⅓	6	4	3	1	0
Drews	2	1	0	0	1	0
Page (L)	1	4	4	4	0	1
Newsom	⅔	1	0	0	0	0
Raschi	1	0	0	0	0	1
Wensloff	2	0	0	0	0	0

CHAPTER

4

1975

Boston Red Sox

vs.

Cincinnati Reds

The Brawl at
the Wall

Interference? Ed Armbrister collides with Boston catcher Carlton Fisk after Armbrister dropped down a bunt. Ump Larry Barnett ruled no interference, and the controversial call influenced the course of the World Series. (AP/Wide World Photos)

Luis Tiant baffled the Reds with knuckleballs, forkballs, screwballs, and a few pitches nobody had ever heard of. (AP/Wide World Photos)

They call it The Green Monster, or sometimes just the Wall. It's the enormous leftfield fence at Fenway Park in Boston.

A towering 37 feet, 2 inches high, the Monster sits 315 feet from home plate. Good hitters treat it like their personal handball court. Weak hitters are so tempted to hit baseballs over it that they swing too hard and hit nothing. Pitchers feel like it's lurking right behind them, breathing down their necks, just waiting to swallow a hanging curveball.

The Green Monster makes Fenway Park a hitter's paradise, where a three-run lead can evaporate while you reach under your seat for your Pepsi. The Monster giveth, and the Monster taketh away.

"I'm not going to look at that fence," said pitcher Don Gullet, who would be starting Game 1 of the World Series for the Cincinnati Reds. "You make a mistake, it can hurt you."

"It looks close," said Cincinnati first baseman Tony Perez. "I've never seen anything like it."

Perez and his Cincinnati teammates were licking their lips in anticipation. They were the "Big Red Machine," the most powerful offensive team in baseball. Catcher Johnny Bench had slugged 28 home runs, leftfielder George Foster hit 23, and Perez had 20. Third baseman Pete Rose hit .317, leading the league in doubles and runs scored. Second baseman Joe Morgan, just five-foot-seven, won the National League Most Valuable Player award with these numbers: .327, 17 homers, 109 RBIs and 67 stolen bases. He also led the league in walks. Rightfielder Ken Griffey hit .305. Shortstop Dave Concepcion hit .274 and stole 33 bases.

None of the Cincinnati pitchers won 16 games. But who needs pitching with a lineup like that? You could almost hear the balls crashing off and over the Wall, and the World Series hadn't even begun.

The Red Sox weren't quite as impressive a team. Their leader was Hall of Famer Carl Yastrzemski, but the surprise sensation of the season had been rookie centerfielder Fred Lynn. By hitting .331 with 21 homers and 105 RBIs, Lynn became the first player ever to win both the Rookie of the Year and Most Valuable Player Awards. He also led the league in runs (103), slugging percentage (.556), doubles (47), and he won the Gold Glove for his spectacular play in centerfield. What a season!

The third outfielder was Dwight Evans, perhaps the best rightfielder in the game. The infield was patrolled by Cecil Cooper at first (.311), Denny Doyle at second (.310 with 21 doubles), Rick Burleson (.252) at short, and Rico Petrocelli at third (.239). Behind the plate was Carlton Fisk. He had a serious knee injury in 1974 and got hurt again during spring training, but came back to hit .331 the second half of the season and .417 in the American League playoffs.

The Sox had the edge in starting pitching, with Rick Wise (19–12), Luis Tiant (18–14) and Bill Lee (17–9).

The fans of Cincinnati and Boston had been waiting for a World Championship for a long time. The Reds had won pennants in 1970 and 1972, but Cincinnati hadn't won the big one since 1940. For Bostonians, the wait was even longer. To remember the taste of World Series victory, they had to think back to 1918, when Babe Ruth pitched for the Red Sox.

One of these teams was going to break its World Series losing streak. The other would have to keep waiting.

GAME 1. Fenway Park was filled with 35,205 fans, and more were hanging perilously off billboards outside the ballpark.

"Loo-ee! Loo-ee! Loo-ee! Loo-ee!" chanted the crowd. They were chanting for balding, chubby, Cuban exile Luis Tiant, the starting pitcher for the Red Sox. He didn't look much like a professional baseball player, but Tiant had averaged 20 victories a year for the last three seasons. Next to Carl Yastrzemski, he was Boston's biggest hero.

El Tiante, as he was called, was anywhere from 35 to 40 years old and no longer had an overpowering fastball. He threw slow junk—knuckleballs, forkballs, screwballs, and a few pitches nobody ever heard of.

When Tiant went into his windup, he would hesitate, turn around, and twitch. Suddenly the ball would appear out of nowhere. He didn't look toward the plate at all; at one point he faced second base. It was a mystery how he ever got a ball over the plate. But he struck out twice as many hitters as he walked in 1975.

This would be a special day for Luis Tiant. The first ball of the World Series was thrown out by his dad, whom he hadn't seen in years. Luis Tiant, Sr., had been a pitching star in Cuba. One day in 1935, he pitched both games of a doubleheader against a team of American stars and held Babe Ruth to one single. It took a special agreement between Cuban dictator Fidel Castro and the U.S. State Department to bring Tiant to America so he could watch his son pitch in the World Series.

He wasn't disappointed. Tiant baffled the Cincinnati Reds. One by one they came to the plate. One by one they were retired with a weak grounder or harmless fly ball.

The Boston hitters weren't doing much better against Don Gullett, the 24-year-old ace of the Cincinnati pitching staff. Gullett had missed two months of the season with a broken thumb but still won 15 games.

After six innings, the scoreboard was a bunch of zeroes.

Luis Tiant led off the seventh inning for the Red Sox. Because of the designated-hitter rule, Tiant hadn't been to bat in three years. But pitchers were required to hit in the World Series in 1975, and Tiant looked fat and rusty.

But on a two strike forkball, Tiant managed to get the bat on the ball and stroke a single. Boston leadoff hitter Dwight Evans was instructed to bunt to advance Tiant to second. He did, and pitcher Don Gullett grabbed the ball quickly. Gullett knew Tiant wasn't used to running bases, so he decided to try and nail him at second. But Gullett, who was used to playing on AstroTurf, slipped on the Fenway Park grass as he turned to throw. The ball skittered away and both runners were safe.

Boston runners on first and second. Nobody out. Second baseman Denny Doyle was up for the Sox. If Doyle could lay down a bunt, the runners would advance to second and third. He tried twice, but fouled the ball each time. The bunt sign was taken off and Doyle got permission to swing away. This time he hit the ball fairly. It snuck between third base and shortstop into leftfield.

Now the bases were loaded with nobody out. This was Boston's big chance. Their big man, Carl Yastrzemski, was up. Yaz was a 15-year veteran and had won three American League batting titles. He ripped a single to right.

Luis Tiant was so unfamiliar with running the bases that he missed the plate scampering home. He had to go back and touch it. Sox 1, Reds 0. The bases were still loaded with nobody out; this had all the makings of a big inning for Boston.

Cincinnati manager Sparky Anderson walked out to the mound. His nickname was Captain Hook, because he removed pitchers as soon as they got into trouble. Sparky decided to lift Don Gullett and bring in reliever Clay Carroll from the Cincinnati bullpen.

The first hitter to face Carroll was 27-year-old catcher

Carlton Fisk. Boston fans called him by his childhood nickname—Pudge. Fisk worked the count until it was full and then gladly watched ball four. That forced in a run, and Boston's lead increased to 2–0. And the Red Sox still had the bases loaded with nobody out.

Captain Hook had seen enough of Clay Carroll. He summoned left-handed sinkerballer Will McEnaney to put out the fire. McEnaney had appeared in 70 games during the season, saving 15 of them and winning 5.

He struck out Fred Lynn, but Boston third baseman Rico Petrocelli grounded a single to leftfield. Two more Red Sox crossed the plate, making it 4–0. Rick Burleson, the Boston shortstop, slapped a single in the same spot and another run scored. Sox 5, Reds 0.

There was only one out, and Boston had runners at first and third. First baseman Cecil Cooper was up. Cooper had been hit in the face by a pitch in September, putting a damper on a great .310 season. He lifted a fly ball deep enough to allow Petrocelli to tag up from third base. That made it 6–0.

"Loo-ee! Loo-ee!" screamed the Fenway crowd. Luis Tiant, who had started the rally with a single, was up again. This time he fouled out to first base and the Cincinnati Reds staggered off the field, stunned and six runs behind.

That was how it ended. Tiant never let up, pitching a complete game, a five-hit shutout. The mighty Big Red Machine had been shut down, turned off, and sold for scrap. The heart of their lineup—Pete Rose, Johnny Bench, and Tony Perez—had gone 0 for 12. Some of the Reds had hit the ball on the nose, but always right at somebody.

"If I didn't count," said Rose after the game, "I'd swear they had 15 fielders out there."

Luis Tiant puffed a big cigar and iced his famous right elbow. "This was my biggest day in eleven years of baseball," he told reporters. "Always I want to be in a World Series, and now is my chance."

The feared Green Monster also had a great day. Not a single baseball reached it the entire game.

GAME 2. It was a rainy day in Boston. Jack Billingham was the Cincinnati starter. He had won 19 games each of the last two seasons, then slumped to 15–10 in 1975.

On the mound for Boston was left-hander Bill Lee, also known as Spaceman. Lee was famous more for his personality than his pitching. When he walked on the field at Fenway Park for the first time and looked at the Wall, he said, "Do they *leave* it there during games?"

Like his teammate Luis Tiant, Bill Lee threw slow junkball pitches. So slow, in fact, that the Cincinnati power hitters were laughing as they watched Lee warm up. But the laughter stopped when Lee struck out Pete Rose to start the game, and blanked the Reds over the first three innings. Bill Lee could pitch. He won 17 games the last three seasons in a row.

*Dwight Evans of the Red Sox takes one on the shoulder in Game 2.
Even catcher Johnny Bench got out of the way. Evans would slam a
homer in Game 3. (AP/Wide World Photos)*

The Red Sox began where they'd left off in Game 1. Cecil Cooper hit Billingham's first pitch to leftfield. George Foster misjudged the ball and it fell in for a double. Denny Doyle rapped a single off Billingham's glove, advancing Cooper to third. Nobody out. Carl Yastrzemski came to the plate.

The Cincinnati defense moved back. They were willing to give up a run on a ground ball if they could get a double play out of it.

Yaz hit a bouncer back to the box. It was a perfect double play grounder. Billingham whipped the ball to Dave Concepcion at second for one out.

Before throwing the ball on to first, Concepcion glanced toward home and noticed that Cecil Cooper had gotten a late start for the plate. Instead of throwing the ball to first, Concepcion sent it home instead. Johnny Bench put the tag on the sliding Cecil Cooper. Out!

The Reds had achieved their double play, and as a bonus they prevented the run from scoring. It was heads-up play by Dave Concepcion and a baserunning blunder by Cecil Cooper.

Yastrzemski had taken second base on the play. When Carlton Fisk slapped a single to rightfield, Yaz scored. Sox 1, Reds 0. By the time the inning ended, Boston had made three hits, but they only had one run to show for them.

Bill Lee was cruising along until the fourth inning, when he walked Joe Morgan with one out. Johnny Bench hit Lee's next pitch to right center for a single. Runners on first and third. When Tony Perez grounded into a force play, Morgan came home. It was Cincinnati's first run of the World Series. Sox 1, Reds 1.

Boston scored another run in the sixth inning, when Dave Concepcion fumbled a grounder and Rico Petrocelli singled the run home. Sox 2, Reds 1. Bill Lee held that lead, allowing Cincinnati only four hits through eight innings. If Lee could get three more outs, Boston would lead the World Series two games to none.

Johnny Bench was set to lead off the ninth inning when the Boston sky darkened and it began to rain. During the rain delay, Bench was interviewed on national television. He told about 50 million people that he was going to stop trying to pull Bill Lee's pitches. Instead, he would attempt to hit the ball to the opposite field.

Nobody bothered telling Bill Lee. Lee figured Bench would be gunning for the Green Monster, so he threw his first pitch on the outside part of the plate. Bench went with the pitch, clubbing an opposite field double in the rightfield corner.

The tying run was in scoring position and the dangerous Tony Perez was up. Boston manager Darrell Johnson decided that eight innings of pitching and a long rain delay had worn Lee out. He brought in Dick Drago, Boston's hard-throwing bullpen ace.

"Man on second base, Dick," said Johnson. "Let's go. Tell you what: Hard. In and out. Up and down. Come on."

Drago got Perez on a bouncer to short. One out. Johnny Bench advanced to third on the play. He was not a fast runner, so Cincinnati would need a long fly ball to score Bench and tie the game up.

The batter was George Foster, a guy who was known to hit a long fly ball now and then. Foster would hit 52 home runs in 1977, making him only the seventh National Leaguer to hit more than 50 in a season.

Drago had two strikes on Foster when the slugger hit a fly ball. It sailed to leftfield, but not deep enough to score Bench from third.

Two outs. One more and the Red Sox would be two games ahead, leaving the Big Red Machine sputtering.

Dave Concepcion was up. He hit a seeing-eye grounder over the mound. Bench broke for the plate. Red Sox second baseman Denny Doyle stopped the ball. If he could make the play at first, Game 2 would be over.

Safe! The game was tied. Sox 2, Reds 2.

It was Ken Griffey's turn. Now the Reds had the chance to win. Griffey fouled off two fastballs, and on the next pitch slammed a double to the wall in left centerfield. Concepcion scored, and suddenly it was Reds 3, Sox 2.

Boston got their last licks in the bottom of the ninth. Facing them was rookie Rawly Eastwick, who had started the season in the minors and was finishing it in the World Series. Eastwick saved 22 games during the season.

Make that 23. He retired the Sox in order in the ninth to end the game.

Afterwards, reporters asked Red Sox pitcher Bill Lee for his general impression of the Series so far.

"Tied," he replied.

GAME 3. If you wanted to pick the ballpark least like Fenway Park, it would have to be Riverfront Stadium in Cincinnati. It holds a lot more people (55,392 were admitted to Game 3), the fences in left and rightfield are the same distance, and the field is covered with artificial turf. The Reds loved the place—they won 64 games and only lost 17 there during the regular season.

The Green Monster had upset everybody's expectations in Game 1 and Game 2. Not a single home run was hit in Fenway Park. Strangely enough, six homers would be hit in Game 3, and Riverfront is a pitcher's ballpark.

Before the game, Sparky Anderson graciously gave Boston manager Darrell Johnson a guided tour around the field. Gary Nolan would be starting for Cincinnati. After missing the entire 1974 season because of shoulder problems, he came back to win 15 games and lead the National League in fewest walks per nine innings (1.24). For Boston, it would be Rick Wise (19–12). One of the best-hitting pitchers in baseball, Wise slugged six homers one year. On one spectacular day in 1971, he tossed a no-hitter and also hit two home runs.

For the third game in a row, Boston drew first blood. In the second inning, catcher Carlton Fisk started the homer parade when he slammed a 1–1 pitch over the leftfield wall. The solo shot put the Red Sox in the lead, 1–0.

The Reds struck back in the fourth inning. With two out, Tony Perez walked and stole second. Johnny Bench followed with a tremendous shot over the left centerfield wall. Reds 2, Sox 1.

The home run barrage continued in the fifth inning. Dave Concepcion slammed one, and centerfielder Cesar Geronimo came up next and hit another one. The back-to-back blasts put Cincinnati in front 4–1. The Reds weren't finished, either. Pete Rose tripled to center and a sacrifice fly by Joe Morgan drove him in.

By the time the inning was over, Boston was on its third pitcher and Cincinnati had rolled up a 5–1 lead. The fans in Riverfront were screaming, and things were looking pretty bad for the Red Sox.

The Sox got one of those runs back on two walks and a wild pitch in the sixth. The next inning, former Cincinnati Red Bernie Carbo slammed a pinch-hit homer over the leftfield wall to reduce Cincinnati's lead to 5–3. As he came off the mound, Reds relief pitcher Clay Carroll threw his glove against the back of the dugout wall with disgust.

Ninth inning. Cincinnati still had a two-run lead, but the Red Sox could be explosive. Rico Petrocelli singled to center, bringing the tying run to the plate—Dwight Evans. Sparky Anderson trotted out of the Reds dugout. He wanted his relief ace Rawly Eastwick to face Evans.

It wasn't such a good idea. Evans got all of an Eastwick

pitch and deposited it over the leftfield wall. When he realized the ball was gone, Evans threw both hands in the air. After being down 5–1, the Red Sox had tied the game up at 5–5. Time for extra innings.

Carl Yastrzemski took matters into his own hands in the tenth when he blasted a shot to straightaway centerfield. But Riverfront Stadium has a lot of running room, and Cesar Geronimo hauled the ball down at the fence.

Geronimo led off in the bottom of the tenth, grounding a single up the middle. It was pitcher Rawly Eastwick's turn to bat, and Sparky Anderson sent up Ed Armbrister—a .185 hitter on the year—to pinch hit.

Andy Warhol once said that in the future everyone would be famous for 15 minutes. Ed Armbrister's time had come.

Jim Willoughby was on the mound for Boston. Armbrister's assignment was to lay down a bunt to advance the runner to second base. Willoughby kept the ball high to make it harder to bunt, but Armbrister got his bat on it.

The ball hit the dirt in front of the plate and bounced about shoulder high. Armbrister, a right-handed hitter, hesitated momentarily in the batter's box. He wasn't sure if the bunt was fair or foul.

"Fair! Fair! In play!" shouted the umpire Larry Barnett.

Red Sox catcher Carlton Fisk charged forward. He grabbed the ball on the first bounce, colliding with Armbrister. Fisk disengaged from Armbrister and whipped the ball to second base, hoping to get the lead runner.

He didn't. The ball sailed over everything. Armbrister made it all the way to second and Geronimo advanced to third.

Darrell Johnson stormed out of the Red Sox dugout. "The man ran into him!" he screamed at umpire Barnett. "The runner was all over the catcher! I'm telling you the man interfered!" Barnett insisted that Armbrister had tried to get out of Fisk's way, so it wasn't interference.

In truth, it doesn't matter what Armbrister tried to do. Rule 7.08b in the baseball rulebook states simply: "A runner who is adjudged to have hindered a fielder who is attempting to make a play on a batted ball is out

Another view of the controversial Armbrister-Fisk collision, showing Fisk about to try for the forced play at second base. His throw sailed into centerfield. (NBL)

whether it was intentional or not." Armbrister should have been called out, and Geronimo returned to first base.

But umpires rarely change their minds, even when they're wrong. Cincinnati had runners on second and third with nobody out and Pete Rose coming up. If they could score a run, the game would be over. The Boston outfielders moved in for a possible play at the plate.

Darrell Johnson, still furious, brought in left-handed sidearmer Roger Moret (14–3). He walked Pete Rose to load the bases. Nobody out. Merv Rettenmund was sent up to pinch hit. Rettenmund could win the game with a hit, a walk, a deep fly ball, a weak grounder, an error— just about anything but a strikeout.

Roger Moret struck him out. One out.

It was Joe Morgan's turn. A double play would get the Red Sox out of the inning.

But Morgan was not feeling cooperative. He lifted a long fly ball to center. Fred Lynn was playing shallow, hoping to cut off the inning run at the plate. Morgan's drive went over his head. Lynn didn't even chase it. The game was over. Reds 6, Sox 5.

WE WIN! announced a message on the scoreboard, as if there were a person in the ballpark who didn't know it already.

There were six home runs, but the game was decided by a bunt that didn't travel five feet. As they came off the field, the Red Sox were furious. They had lost Game 2 in the ninth inning, and now Game 3 had been stolen from them because of a botched call in the tenth inning. It could have been a three game lead for Boston. Instead, Cincinnati was ahead two games to one. Sometimes life isn't fair.

GAME 4. "Nobody wanted to leave the ballpark last night," Red Sox second baseman Denny Doyle said on the morning of Game 4. "We wanted to turn around halfway to the hotel, come back and play another one after losing like that. The longest day I ever spent was waiting to come out here today."

Game 4 didn't start off so well for the Red Sox either. Luis Tiant was their starter again, and Pete Rose greeted him with a ground single up the middle. Rose was running on the first pitch to Ken Griffey, who clubbed the ball to left centerfield. Rose scored, and the Reds were ahead, 1–0.

After pitching nine shutout innings in Game 1, Tiant had given up a run in the first inning. It could be another long day.

Griffey tried to stretch his hit into a triple and was thrown out at third. But Tiant walked Joe Morgan, and Johnny Bench ripped a double to right center to score him. Reds 2, Sox 0. The pitching mound at Riverfront Stadium seemed lower than the one Tiant was used to at Fenway Park. It was hurting his control and forcing him to use his fastball more frequently.

Cincinnati starter Fred Norman kept the Sox bats quiet until the fourth inning, when they erupted. Carlton Fisk and Fred Lynn singled with one out. They moved to second and third on a wild pitch. Dwight Evans slammed a double to the rightfield fence to score both of them and tie the game. Reds 2, Sox 2.

On the next pitch, Rick Burleson hit a line drive to the left side. Shortstop Dave Concepcion leaped for it, but the ball zipped over his glove. Dwight Evans scooted home, putting the Red Sox in the lead, 3–2. Burleson alertly took second base when centerfielder Cesar Geronimo took his time throwing the ball in.

That was all for Fred Norman. Pedro Borbon came in to pitch for Cincinnati. Borbon was famous for his unusual warm up routine—he liked to stand on the warning track in centerfield and throw strikes to home plate. He only did that during practice, of course.

Luis Tiant was the batter. He continued his hot hitting (he would hit .250 for the Series) with a single to center. That put Boston runners at first and third. Juan Beniquez tapped a slow roller down the first baseline, but Tony Perez fumbled the ball. Burleson scored on the play, making it 4–2. Carl Yastrzemski kept the rally going with a single to right, driving in Tiant. That was the sixth Boston hit of inning, and the Red Sox were in front, 5–2.

But in the bottom half of the inning, Cincinnati came right back. With two outs and nobody on, George Foster got an infield single. Dave Concepcion hit a little looper to left. Three Red Sox fielders went after the ball, but it fell between them for a double. Foster, who was running on anything, came all the way around to score. Sox 5, Reds 3. When Geronimo followed with a triple in the left-field corner, it was 5–4.

After surrendering four runs over the first four innings, Luis Tiant finally found his groove. Tiant did a little dancing in and out of trouble, but he kept the Reds off the scoreboard in the fifth, sixth, seventh, and eighth innings. Three more outs and the Series would be tied up.

Cesar Geronimo led off the final inning with a single, just as he had in Game 3. It was his third hit of the game. A pinch hitter stepped out of the Cincinnati dugout and the crowd cheered when they realized it was . . . Ed Armbrister. Yesterday's dubious hero was sent in to bunt Geronimo over to second.

Not again! The Red Sox remembered the controversial bunt that defeated them the day before.

Armbrister got his bunt down again, but this time he ran to first quickly and there was no collison. The sacrifice advanced Geronimo to second.

On the mound, Luis Tiant shook his head. The heart of the Big Red Machine was coming up—Pete Rose, Ken Griffey, and Joe Morgan. All three would be hitting left-handed.

Darrell Johnson walked to the mound, and it looked like Tiant's day might be over. The Sox infield gathered to listen.

"What do you guys think?" Johnson asked the group. "I've got a left-hander down there, Luis. Can you get him?"

Tiant said he could. Johnson decided to gamble and leave Tiant in the game. "Get after him good," he said before returning to the Boston dugout. "Come on."

But Tiant walked Pete Rose. Now the tying and winning runs were on base. Darrell Johnson came out of the Boston dugout again. Tiant was certain to be replaced.

"How do you feel?" Johnson asked Tiant.

"He's still throwing good," said catcher Carlton Fisk. Once more, Johnson decided to stick with Tiant. He was the best Boston had.

Ken Griffey came to the plate. He and Tiant dueled until the count reached three balls and two strikes. The crowd at Riverfront began clapping rhythmically.

Tiant threw and Griffey swung, drilling a shot to centerfield. Fred Lynn misjudged the ball at first. If it sailed over his head to the wall, Geronimo and Rose would score to win the game for Cincinnati.

Lynn turned his back and sprinted for the wall. At the warning track, he reached over his head at the last instant and made an incredible catch. Two outs. The runners raced back to first and second.

Tiant still had to worry about Joe Morgan, perhaps the toughest out in baseball.

With a 1–0 count, Sparky Anderson put on the hit-and-run play. The runners broke with the pitch. Morgan swung and got the bat on the ball. But not much bat. He popped the ball up toward the right side of the infield. Yastrzemski drifted over and grabbed it.

That's the ballgame. Sox 5, Reds 4.

Luis Tiant's old right arm had thrown 163 pitches, but he managed to beat the Reds narrowly for his second victory of the World Series.

It was all tied up, two games apiece.

GAME 5. Don Gullett had been masterful in Game 1, shutting out the Red Sox for six innings. Then the roof fell in and the Sox beat him by the score of 6–0. Now Gullett, a farm boy from Kentucky, would get another chance. He was determined not to blow it.

Gullett was looking shaky in the first inning. Boston second baseman Denny Doyle crashed a triple and Carl Yastrzemski drove him in with a sacrifice fly. Boston 1, Reds 0. But after that, Gullett settled down and Boston hitters were virtually helpless against him.

Reggie Cleveland was mowing down the Cincinnati hitters through the first three innings, but nobody could hold the Big Red Machine for long. In the fourth, Tony Perez jumped all over a Cleveland slider that was up around the letters with nothing on it.

As the ball sailed over the left centerfield fence, Perez clapped his hands together with delight. He was a streak hitter, and he had been 0 for 15 through the first four games of the World Series. Maybe now the streak was over. Sox 1, Reds 1.

Cincinnati made it 2–1 in the fifth when Gullett singled and Pete Rose doubled.

In the sixth, facing Jim Willoughby, they did some real damage. Joe Morgan started things off by walking. With Johnny Bench at the plate, Boston pitcher Reggie Cleveland threw over to first base 16 times trying to hold Morgan on. Then Cincinnati put on the hit-and-run. Joe Morgan broke for second. As Boston second baseman Denny Doyle went to cover the bag, Bench leaned over the plate and punched the ball right through the spot vacated by Doyle. Morgan made it to third and Bench to second.

That brought up Tony Perez, still feeling a surge of confidence from his homer in the fourth inning. On a 1–2 count, he popped a foul ball behind the plate. Boston catcher Carlton Fisk dove into the photographer's box trying for the ball, but missed it by inches. On the next pitch Perez hit the ball in fair territory—deep over the left centerfield fence. It was his second home run of the game, and this one went even further than the first one.

When Perez was cold, he was cold as ice. But now he was hot, and he was smoking. Reds 5, Sox 1.

That was more than enough for Don Gullett. He was working on a two-hit masterpiece before tiring in the ninth inning. Rawly Eastwick came in and struck out Rico Petrocelli on three pitches to end the game.

Final score: Reds 6, Sox 2.

Now Cincinnati was leading the Series three games to two. One more win and the World Championship would be theirs. It was back to Boston for Game 6, which would turn out to be one of the most memorable baseball games ever played.

GAME 6.   It was raining in Boston when the Reds and Red Sox arrived on Friday, October 17. The field was unplayable on Saturday. It rained again on Sunday, and again on Monday. It seemed as though it would never stop raining. It was as if Somebody up there didn't want the World Series to end.

Players on both teams got edgy. Cincinnati wanted to get Game 6 over with and claim their crown. Boston was itching for one last chance to save the season.

Finally, on Tuesday, October 21, the sky cleared. A gorgeous full moon hovered above Fenway Park, like a fly ball that refused to come down.

The three days of rain provided one advantage for the Red Sox—it gave Luis Tiant's old right arm time to recover from the 163 pitches he threw in Game 4. Tiant had already won two games. The crowd was chanting *"Loo-ee! Loo-ee!"* as he walked to the mound once again. Tiant calmly disposed of Rose (fly to left), Morgan (foul pop), and Bench (strikeout) in the first inning.

Gary Nolan was the Cincinnati starter. Boston had knocked him out after four innings in Game 3. Nolan wouldn't make it past two innings tonight.

He retired the first two Red Sox out in the first inning, but then Carl Yastrzemski and Carlton Fisk each rapped a single past the infield. As he stepped into the batter's box, Fred Lynn glanced at the runners on first and second. Norman's first pitch was out of the strike zone, but Lynn liked the next one and took a healthy cut. He got all of it, and it sailed over the Boston bullpen in right centerfield. Yastrzemski and Fisk gleefully crossed the plate, followed by Fred Lynn. Just like that, Boston had jumped in front, 3–0.

In the third inning, the Red Sox had the chance to deliver the knockout punch. They loaded the bases on a double and two walks, but Jack Billingham fanned Rico Petrocelli with a curveball to end the threat.

Luis Tiant was hanging goose eggs on the Reds through the first four innings. In the fifth he walked pinch hitter Ed Armbrister and gave up a full count single to Pete Rose. Ken Griffey—the tying run—was at the plate.

With the count two balls and two strikes, Griffey connected. The ball shot to straightway centerfield, which of course is the deepest part of any ballpark. Centerfield Fred Lynn knew immediately that the ball was going a long way. He turned his back to the plate and sprinted for the wall. When he ran out of running room, Lynn jumped.

The ball hit the concrete wall. Lynn hit the concrete wall. Baseballs survive these collisions better than people do. The ball bounced away, while Lynn slumped to the ground.

Armbrister and Rose flew around the bases. By the time the Red Sox got the ball in, Ken Griffey was standing on third. Now it was Sox 3, Reds 2.

After five minutes of hushed silence in Fenway Park, Fred Lynn slowly, unsteadily struggled to his feet. He had been hurt badly, but he stayed in the game. After all, this could be the final game of the season. His body would have five months to heal.

Meanwhile, the Red Sox still had Johnny Bench to contend with, and a runner on third base. Bench took care of that. He smashed Tiant's first pitch off the Green Monster. Ken Griffey trotted home and very quickly the Reds had tied it up at 3–3.

Ken Griffey was up again to lead off the seventh inning. He got another hit, a single to right. Joe Morgan followed with single too. Tiant managed to retire Johnny Bench and Tony Perez on fly balls, but George Foster launched a cannon shot to the centerfield. This time Fred Lynn wisely chose to play the ball off the wall. Griffey and Morgan scored, and it was Reds 5, Sox 3.

In the next inning Cesar Geronimo led off for Cincinnati and slammed Tiant's first pitch into the rightfield stands. It was his second home run of the Series.

That made it Reds 6, Sox 3. Luis Tiant, who had pitched marvelously in three games, had finally been knocked out of the box. Roger Moret replaced him and put out the fire.

The Red Sox were down to their last six outs. They hadn't put a run on the scoreboard since the first inning, and they needed three just to tie the game. It looked hopeless. The season was surely coming to an end for Boston.

In the bottom of the eighth inning, they would face Pedro Borbon, Cincinnati's fifth pitcher of the game. The indestructable Fred Lynn led off, smashing a line drive that ricocheted off Borbon's leg. Lynn made it safely to first. Borbon walked Rico Petrocelli. Runners at first and second, nobody out. Dwight Evans stepped to the plate, knowing full well that he could tie the game with a homer.

Sparky Anderson wasn't taking any chances. He brought in Rawly Eastwick, who had been the winner in Game 2 and Game 3.

Evans and Eastwick had faced each other in the ninth inning of Game 3. That time, Evans hit a two-run homer that sent the game into extra innings. The law of averages says Evans isn't going to hit a homer off Eastwick again.

The law was right. This time, Eastwick struck out Evans. One out.

Eastwick got Rick Burleson on a fly ball to left for the second out. Four more outs and the Cincinnati Reds would win the World Series.

It was pitcher Roger Moret's turn to bat, but there was no way he was going to get the chance to hit in such a crucial situation. Instead, pinch hitter Bernie Carbo stepped out of the Boston dugout.

In his last at bat, back in Game 3, Carbo had slammed a home run. The law of averages says he won't pinch hit two homers in two consecutive at-bats.

It was a fastball pitcher against a fastball hitter.

Eastwick got a two-strike advantage on Carbo, then threw two pitches off the plate to even the count. Carbo awkwardly fouled off a slider. Catcher Johnny Bench signaled for a fastball to cross Carbo up, and Carbo guessed that Bench would call for a fastball to cross him up.

The pitch came in a little high, and Carbo swiped at it. The crack of the bat was all it took for Fenway Park to realize Bernie Carbo had tied the game. It was a tremendous home run into the centerfield bleachers. Lynn, Petrocelli, and Carbo danced around the bases. They were mobbed at home plate by the rest of the Red Sox.

Sox 6, Reds 6. Fenway Park sounded like a jet taking off. So much for the law of averages.

The Red Sox were almost dead when Bernie Carbo unloaded this three-run blast off Rawly Eastwick to tie Game 6 in the bottom of the eighth inning. (AP/Wide World Photos)

Cincinnati went down in order in the top of the ninth. In the bottom of the ninth, the Red Sox loaded the bases with nobody out. Incredibly, they could not score.

The game went into extra innings. Chances were the next team to score would win the game. The tension grew when neither team could push a run across the plate in the tenth.

Pete Rose stepped into the batter's box to start the eleventh. Before the first pitch came in, he turned to Boston catcher Carlton Fisk.

"This is some kind of game, isn't it?" Rose asked.

Rose was nicked by a pitch from new reliever Dick Drago. The winning run was on first, with nobody out. Ken Griffey tried to bunt Rose over, but Fisk grabbed the ball and whipped it to second for the force play. One out. Ken Griffey replaced Rose at first.

Joe Morgan was up. Drago went into his windup and Morgan rocketed a vicious line drive to rightfield. It looked like it could be the World Series-winning homer. Ken Griffey raced around the bases.

Dwight Evans, an eight-time Gold Glove winner, ran back and to his right. He didn't have much time because the ball had been hit so hard. A stride from the low outfield wall, Evans desperately stabbed his glove over his head.

It was a miracle catch. Somehow, the ball found Evans's glove. Somehow, it stayed there when he crashed into the low wall. Two outs.

The play was even more remarkable because after he caught the ball Dwight Evans had the presense of mind to throw it to first base. Double play! Three outs! End of inning.

Pat Darcy came in and retired Boston 1–2–3 in the eleventh. Rick Wise held the Reds scoreless in the top of the twelfth.

First the Sox had a three-run lead, then the Reds tied it up. Then the Reds had a three-run lead, and the Sox tied it up. Twelve pitchers had been to the mound. The game was entering its fifth hour.

Nobody in Fenway Park was getting up from his seat to beat the traffic. Television sets were turning on across America. People had heard a great game was in progress and they wanted to see how it turned out.

Carlton Fisk would lead off the bottom of the twelfth for the Red Sox. Fisk had hit a homer in Game 3, but his throwing error had cost the Sox that game. He remembered it.

In the on-deck circle, Fisk said to Fred Lynn, "Freddy, I'm gonna hit one off the wall. You drive me in."

"Sounds good to me," Lynn replied as Fisk strode to the batter's box.

Pat Darcy looked in for the sign from Johnny Bench. The pitch was high, and Fisk watched it go by. Ball one.

Bench signaled for a sinkerball, low and inside. Darcy kicked up his leg and pitched. He made a good pitch. It would have hit Bench's glove. Instead, it hit Fisk's bat. Hard.

It was a long, high drive, not a line drive, down the left-field line. All eyes turned toward the Green Monster. For a moment that seemed to last forever, the ball was over the lights of Fenway and out of sight.

Fisk took a step toward first base and stopped. There was no point in running. The shot was either the game-winning home run or a meaningless foul ball. Instinctively, Fisk waved his arms to urge the ball fair, like someone directing planes on a runway. It's called using body English.

They say baseball is a game of inches. If Fisk's drive landed an inch to the left of the foul pole, it would be a foul ball. An inch to the right, and it would be a home run. And according to the rules of baseball, any ball that hits the foul pole itself counts as a home run.

Finally, the baseball reappeared. It plummeted for an instant, and then, as if Hollywood had written the ending, it ticked off Fenway Park's yellow foul pole.

Home run! The Red Sox had beaten the Reds 7–6 and tied up the World Series.

Carlton Fisk jumped up in the air, threw his hands over his head and skipped around the bases like a kid who woke up on the day of the big test to find a foot of snow on the ground. Fisk had to muscle his way past third base, bowling over fans who had climbed on the field in an

If Carlton Fisk's drive landed an inch to the left of the foul pole, it would be a strike. An inch to the right, and it would be a game-winning homer. Fisk stood there and waved his arms, urging the ball fair, like someone directing planes on an airport runway. (AP/Wide World Photos)

effort to touch him and capture a piece of the moment. He leaped on home plate with both feet and disappeared beneath the frenzied congratulations of his teammates.

The World Series was tied at three games apiece. Boston hadn't seen anything like it since they held a little tea party for the British back in 1773.

"He's a lowball pitcher," Fisk said about Pat Darcy after the game. "I'm a lowball, dead-pull hitter, so I was looking for that one pitch in that one area. I got it, then drove it. I knew it was going to be foul or a home run. I don't think I've ever gone through a more emotional game."

Cincinnati manager Sparky Anderson described it as "like being in an ax fight and finishing second."

Fisk leaps on home plate and is pummeled by teammates and fans. It looked like the end of the World Series . . . but there was one more game to play. (AP/Wide World Photos)

GAME 7. A baseball season is long. There's a month of spring training, followed by 162 games, and if you're lucky, the playoffs and World Series. After all that, it can come down to this. One game. Winner take all.

"We're playing for one thing," said Pete Rose before the game, "those diamond rings."

After Carlton Fisk's miracle home run the night before, the underdog Red Sox were finally the favorites. They had the momentum. They also had home field advantage, which is considerable when 35,000 Bostonians are screaming and the Green Monster is lurking.

"I'm riding with my number-one horse," said Cincinnati manager Sparky Anderson. He was referring to Don Gullett, who had beaten Boston with a sparkling five-hitter in Game 5. Bill Lee, who had pitched eight strong innings in a losing effort in Game 2, would start for Boston.

Seventy-six million people would watch Game 7 on television. They saw no fireworks until the bottom of the third inning. With one out, Gullett walked Bernie Carbo. Denny Doyle, who had made a hit in every game of the Series, singled to right. Boston had runners at first and third.

Carl Yastrzemski grounded a single into rightfield, and Carbo jogged home with the first run of the game. Yaz scampered to second base on the throw. The Sox had runners at second and third now, with Carlton Fisk coming up.

Everybody in America remembered what Fisk had done in the twelfth inning the night before. It wasn't a big surprise that Gullett gave Fisk an intentional walk. That loaded the bases for Fred Lynn, who had a chance to dig

Cincinnati's grave. A poke over the Green Monster would send Boston in front by the score of 5–0.

But Don Gullett would have no part of that. He snuck a called third strike past Lynn for the second out.

That should have settled Gullett down, but he went to a full count on Boston's weakest hitter—Rico Petrocelli— and walked him. That forced in a run and Boston had a 2–0 lead. Still the bases were loaded.

Gullett was losing his composure. Dwight Evans was up. He watched the first pitch sail out of the strike zone for ball one. Another pitch was off the plate. Ball two. Evans probably figured he might as well just stand there and see if Gullett could get the ball over.

He couldn't. The next two pitches missed the strike zone as well. That was Gullett's fourth walk of the inning. Evans trotted to first, and another run was forced home. Sox 3, Reds 0. And still the bases were loaded.

Boston fans, anticipating their first World Series victory in 57 years, were screaming for more. The situation was ripe for Gullett to crack, but he summoned up some inner strength that only the best pitchers possess. He struck out Rick Burleson on a curveball to end the inning. Boston had scored three cheap runs on two singles.

Bill Lee was looking sharp, protecting the three-run lead. In the fifth inning, the Reds put runners at first and third with nobody out. But Lee got a strikeout and double play grounder to work his way out of the jam.

Going into the sixth inning, it was the Reds who

had their backs against the wall—the big green wall.

Pete Rose led off with a single. Joe Morgan popped up for the first out. Johnny Bench was up. Lee threw him a fastball low and away. Bench hit a two-hopper toward short. A perfect double play ball.

Burleson fielded the grounder cleanly and threw to second baseman Denny Doyle. Doyle tagged the bag for the second out. As he was pivoting to make his throw to first, a truck named Pete Rose barreled into him. Doyle's throw sailed into the stands. Bench took second on the overthrow.

Because Rose had broken up the double play, Tony Perez would get a chance to hit. Perez was known as a good off-speed hitter. Bill Lee was a junkball pitcher. With the count 1–0, Lee tried to fool Perez with a big, slow, rainbow curve.

Perez was not fooled. He cranked the ball over the left-field screen for his third home run of the Series. That made it Sox 3, Reds 2.

Don Gullett was gone after four innings, and a parade of Cincinnati relievers kept Boston's bats quiet.

In the seventh, Bill Lee developed a blister on his left thumb. Lee, who hadn't issued a base on balls all game, suddenly couldn't get the ball over. He walked Ken Griffey. Red Sox manager Darrell Johnson immediately summoned Roger Moret from the bullpen.

"I was sick with myself," said Bill Lee. "I did not want to come out of that ball game."

Moret retired Cesar Geronimo on an infield pop for the first out. With pinch hitter Ed Armbrister up, Ken Griffey stole second. He didn't have to bother. Armbrister walked, putting Cincinnati runners at first and second.

That brought up Pete Rose, and the man with more singles than anybody in baseball history lined a single to centerfield. Griffey dashed home with the tying run. Sox 3, Reds 3. The Reds couldn't score a go-ahead run, and nobody scored in the eighth inning.

Jim Burton took the mound for the Red Sox. The rookie left-hander had started the season at Pawtucket in the International League. Now he was pitching with the score tied in the ninth inning of the seventh game of the World Series against the mighty Big Red Machine. How's that for pressure?

Burton went to three balls and two strikes on Ken Griffey. The next pitch was high and Griffey walked to first. Cincinnati needed a run to break the tie, so Cesar Geronimo was instructed to bunt Griffey to second. He dropped down a good one. Rico Petrocelli slipped picking up the ball and barely nipped Geronimo at first.

If Burton was nervous, he wasn't showing it. He calmly retired pinch hitter Dan Driessen on a grounder to second. Two outs. Ken Griffey moved to third on the play.

Pete Rose stepped up to the plate. Boston manager Darrell Johnson thought it would be a good time to go out to the mound and chat with his young pitcher.

"Walking this man doesn't bother me a bit," he told

Burton. "This guy's a good fastball hitter. Move the ball around. Shoot for the black."

Burton did as he was told. Rose didn't bite at any of the pitches off the plate, gladly taking a base on balls. That put runners at first and third with two outs. It was Joe Morgan's turn.

Morgan, the National League MVP, wasn't having a great Series. He was hitting a weak .231. Burton got two strikes on him, and Morgan fouled off the next pitch to stay alive.

Burton's next pitch was a slider, low and outside. "It was just about as perfect a pitch that you can make," Burton would tell the press after the game, "exactly where I wanted to put it."

But Joe Morgan didn't hit .327 by striking out on tough pitches. He fought off the slider, poking a flare off the end of his bat.

The ball looped over the Boston infield.

Shortstop Rick Burleson backpedaled frantically.

Centerfielder Fred Lynn charged in.

The ball dropped in front of him.

Ken Griffey crossed the plate, and Cincinnati had the lead for the first time in the game. Reds 4, Sox 3.

Now it was the bottom of the ninth, the last chance for the Red Sox. Will McEnaney was on the mound for Cincinnati.

Boston sent up Juan Beniquez to pinch hit. He hit a line drive to rightfield, but right at Ken Griffey. One out.

Another pinch hitter, Bob Montgomery, was sent up to the plate. He grounded to short and Concepcion made the play flawlessly. Two outs.

The last hope for the Red Sox was Carl Yastrzemski, the heart and soul of Boston. The only other time Yaz had been in the World Series—in 1967—he had made the last out. He didn't want to do it again.

Yastrzemski would slug 452 home runs in his Hall of Fame career. He was probably thinking that he would give them all up to hit one right now and tie the game.

McEnaney went into his windup and the pitch looked good. Yaz swung and hit a high fly to centerfield. Geronimo drifted back.

Yastrzemski knew immediately that the ball wasn't going out. Geronimo squeezed it and "the brawl at the Wall" was over. The Cincinnati Reds had won their first championship since 1940.

"I've waited eleven years for this," said a jubilant Joe Morgan in the clubhouse. "Now I can go home and say I'm on the best team in baseball."

"We didn't win the Series," said Boston pitcher Bill Lee, "but we didn't lose it either. Baseball won. We were part of an event that we could tell our grandchildren about."

For Baseball Trivia Lovers . . .

♦ "I can't wait to get home to watch it again," said Pete Rose after Game 7. The VCR had just been introduced in 1975, and Rose was one of the first to own one.

♦ The World Series might have turned out differently if Boston outfielder Jim Rice had been able to play. Rice had been hit by a pitch that broke his thumb three weeks earlier. With his .309 average, 22 homers, and 102 RBIs, he would have been a force.

♦ Of the 15 classic ballparks built between 1909 and 1923, only four remain today: Fenway Park, Wrigley Field, Tiger Stadium, and Yankee Stadium. They are a true endangered species.

♦ The Green Monster wasn't always green, and it wasn't always a monster. When Fenway Park was built in 1912, it had a regular leftfield wall. The Monster went up in 1933, and it was covered with billboards for Gem razor blades and Lifebuoy soap.

♦ Riverfront Stadium in Cincinnati rests above an enormous underground parking garage. During one game in 1976, there was a "bee delay" when a swarm of bees took over the field.

♦ With ten hits and a .370 average, Pete Rose was the World Series MVP. Everybody knows Rose has more hits than any player in baseball history. He also has more singles (3,215), more at-bats (14,053) and played in more games (3,562). He is the only player to play 500 games at five different positions. It was Yankees pitcher Whitey Ford who nicknamed Rose Charlie Hustle.

♦ In 1968, 21-year-old rookie Johnny Bench asked Ted Williams for an autograph. Williams wrote, "To Johnny Bench, a Hall of Famer for sure. Twenty-one years later,

Johnny Bench was inducted into the Baseball Hall of Fame.

♦ From 1970 to 1977, Cincinnati players won six Most Valuable Player awards: Bench (1970), Bench (1972), Rose (1973), Morgan (1975), Morgan (1976), and Foster (1977).

♦ In 1993, six days after he broke the record for catching more major league games than any other player in baseball history, Carlton Fisk was released by the Chicago White Sox. Fisk, 45 years old, had caught 2,226 games in 22 seasons. He also owns the record for the most home runs hit by a catcher—351.

♦ The World Series losing streak of the Boston Red Sox remains intact to this day. In 1986, they came within one strike of winning the Series, then lost to the New York Mets. As of 1994, it has been 76 years since Boston enjoyed a World Championship.

BOX SCORES

Game 1

Saturday, October 11, At Boston

Cincinnati	AB.	R.	H.	RBI.	PO.	A.
Rose, 3b	4	0	0	0	0	0
Morgan, 2b	4	0	2	0	2	0
Bench, c	4	0	0	0	6	1
Perez, 1b	4	0	0	0	9	0
Foster, lf	4	0	2	0	1	0
Concepcion, ss	4	0	0	0	2	3
Griffey, rf	3	0	1	0	2	0
Geronimo, cf	3	0	0	0	2	1
Gullett, p	3	0	0	0	0	0
Carroll, p	0	0	0	0	0	0
McEnaney, p	0	0	0	0	0	0
Totals	31	0	5	0	24	7

Boston	AB.	R.	H.	RBI.	PO.	A.
Evans, rf	4	1	1	0	4	0
Doyle, 2b	3	1	2	0	3	3
Yastrzemski, lf	4	1	1	1	3	0
Fisk, c	3	1	0	1	4	1
Lynn, cf	4	0	2	0	3	0
Petrocelli, 3b	3	1	2	2	1	3
Burleson, ss	3	0	3	1	1	1
Cooper, 1b	3	0	0	1	8	0
Tiant, p	3	1	1	0	0	0
Totals	30	6	12	6	27	8

```
Cincinnati ..........0 0 0  0 0 0  0 0 0—0
Boston ..............0 0 0  0 0 0  6 0 x—6
```

Cincinnati	IP.	H.	R.	ER.	BB.	SO.
Gullett (L)	6*	10	4	4	4	3
Carroll	0†	1	1	1	1	0
McEnaney	2	2	1	1	1	1

Boston	IP.	H.	R.	ER.	BB.	SO.
Tiant (W)	9	5	0	0	2	3

Game 2

Sunday, October 12, At Boston

Cincinnati	AB.	R.	H.	RBI.	PO.	A.
Rose, 3b	4	0	2	0	1	1
Morgan, 2b	3	1	0	0	0	4
Bench, c	4	1	2	0	9	3
Perez, 1b	3	0	0	1	8	0
Foster, lf	4	0	1	2	0	0
Concepcion, ss	4	1	1	1	2	4
Griffey, rf	4	0	1	1	2	0
Geronimo, cf	3	0	0	0	3	0
Billingham, p	2	0	0	0	0	2
Borbon, p	0	0	0	0	0	0
McEnaney, p	0	0	0	0	0	0
aRettenmund	1	0	0	0	0	0
Eastwick, p	1	0	0	0	0	0
Totals	33	3	7	3	27	14

Boston	AB.	R.	H.	RBI.	PO.	A.
Cooper, 1b	5	0	1	0	10	1
Doyle, 2b	4	0	1	0	2	5
Yastrzemski, lf	3	2	1	0	1	0
Fisk, c	3	0	1	1	5	1
Lynn, cf	4	0	0	0	5	0
Petrocelli, 3b	4	0	2	1	0	0
Evans, rf	2	0	0	0	2	0
Burleson, ss	4	0	1	0	2	4
Lee, p	3	0	0	0	0	0
Drago, p	0	0	0	0	0	0
bCarbo	1	0	0	0	0	0
Totals	33	2	7	2	27	11

```
Cincinnati ..........0 0 0  1 0 0  0 0 2—3
Boston ..............1 0 0  0 0 1  0 0 0—2
```

Cincinnati	IP.	H.	R.	ER.	BB.	SO.
Billingham	5⅓	6	2	1	2	5
Borbon	⅓	0	0	0	0	0
McEnaney	1	0	0	0	0	2
Eastwick (W)	2	1	0	0	0	1

Boston	IP.	H.	R.	ER.	BB.	SO.
Lee	8*	5	2	2	2	5
Drago (L)	1	2	1	1	1	0

Game 3

Tuesday, October 14, At Cincinnati

Boston	AB.	R.	H.	RBI.	PO.	A.
Cooper, 1b	5	0	0	0	14	0
Doyle, 2b	5	0	1	0	0	6
Yastrzemski, lf	4	1	0	0	1	0
Fisk, c	3	1	1	1	5	0
Lynn, cf	3	0	1	0	1	0
Petrocelli, 3b	4	1	2	0	1	5
Evans, rf	4	2	2	1	0	0
Burleson, ss	4	0	2	0	0	1
Wise, p	2	0	0	0	0	0
Burton, p	0	0	0	0	0	0
Cleveland, p	0	0	0	0	0	0
aCarbo	1	1	1	1	0	0
Willoughby, p	0	0	0	0	0	0
Morel, p	0	0	0	0	0	0
Totals	35	5	10	5	28	12

Cincinnati	AB.	R.	H.	RBI.	PO.	A.
Rose, 3b	4	1	1	0	2	1
Griffey, rf	3	0	0	0	1	1
cRettenmund	1	0	0	0	0	0
Morgan, 2b	4	0	1	2	4	5
Perez, 1b	3	1	0	0	13	0
Bench, c	4	1	1	2	2	1
Foster, lf	3	0	0	0	3	0
Concepcion, ss	4	1	1	0	2	5
Geronimo, cf	4	2	2	1	3	0
Nolan, p	1	0	0	0	0	0
Darcy, p	1	0	0	0	0	0
Carroll, p	0	0	0	0	0	0
McEnaney, p	1	0	1	0	0	0
Eastwick, p	0	0	0	0	0	0
bArmbrister	1	0	0	0	0	0
Totals	34	6	7	6	30	14

```
Boston ..............0 1 0  0 0 1  1 0 2—5
Cincinnati ..........0 0 0  2 3 0  0 0 1—6
```
One out when winning run scored.

Boston	IP.	H.	R.	ER.	BB.	SO.
Wise	4⅓	4	5	5	2	1
Burton	⅓	0	0	0	1	0
Cleveland	1⅓	0	0	0	0	2
Willoughby (L)	3†	2	1	0	0	1
Morel	⅓	1	0	0	1	1

Cincinnati	IP.	H.	R.	ER.	BB.	SO.
Nolan	2	3	1	1	1	0
Darcy	2*	2	1	1	2	0
Carroll	¾	1	1	1	0	0
McEnaney	1⅓	1	1	1	0	2
Eastwick (W)	1⅔	3	1	1	0	0

Game 4

Wednesday, October 15, At Cincinnati

Boston	AB.	R.	H.	RBI.	PO.	A.
Beniquez, lf	4	0	1	1	4	0
Miller, lf	1	0	0	0	0	0
Doyle, 2b	5	0	2	0	2	3
Yastrzemski, 1b	4	0	2	1	8	0
Fisk, c	5	1	0	0	4	0
Lynn, cf	4	0	1	0	4	1
Petrocelli, 3b	4	0	1	0	1	1
Evans, rf	4	1	2	2	3	0
Burleson, ss	4	1	1	1	0	2
Tiant, p	3	1	1	0	0	2
Totals	38	5	11	5	27	10

Cincinnati	AB.	R.	H.	RBI.	PO.	A.
Rose, 3b	3	1	1	0	1	3
Griffey, rf	5	0	1	1	0	0
Morgan, 2b	3	1	0	0	2	7
Perez, 1b	4	0	0	0	12	1
Bench, c	4	0	1	1	4	0
Foster, lf	4	1	2	0	0	0
Concepcion, ss	4	1	1	1	3	4
Geronimo, cf	4	0	3	1	4	0
Norman, p	1	0	0	0	0	0
Borbon, p	0	0	0	0	0	0
aCrowley	1	0	0	0	0	0
Carroll, p	0	0	0	0	1	0
bChaney	1	0	0	0	0	0
Eastwick, p	0	0	0	0	0	0
cArmbrister	0	0	0	0	0	0
Totals	34	4	9	4	27	15

```
Boston ..............0 0 0  5 0 0  0 0 0—5
Cincinnati ..........2 0 0  2 0 0  0 0 0—4
```

Boston	IP.	H.	R.	ER.	BB.	SO.
Tiant (W)	9	9	4	4	4	4

Cincinnati	IP.	H.	R.	ER.	BB.	SO.
Norman (L)	3⅓	7	4	4	1	2
Borbon	⅔	2	1	0	0	0
Carroll	2	1	0	0	0	2
Eastwick	3	0	0	0	1	0

BOX SCORES

Game 5

Thursday, October 16, At Cincinnati

Boston	AB.	R.	H.	RBI.	PO.	A.
Beniquez, lf	3	0	0	0	2	1
Doyle, 2b	4	1	1	0	1	1
Yastrzemski, 1b	3	1	1	1	6	0
Fisk, c	4	0	1	0	6	0
Lynn, cf	4	0	1	1	2	0
Petrocelli, 3b	4	0	0	0	2	1
Evans, rf	3	0	1	0	3	0
Burleson, ss	3	0	0	0	1	2
Cleveland, p	2	0	0	0	0	0
Willoughby, p	0	0	0	0	1	0
aGriffin	1	0	0	0	0	0
Pole, p	0	0	0	0	0	0
Segui, p	0	0	0	0	0	0
Totals	31	2	5	2	24	5

Cincinnati	AB.	R.	H.	RBI.	PO.	A.
Rose, 3b	3	0	2	1	1	0
Griffey, rf	4	0	1	0	2	0
Morgan, 2b	3	1	1	0	3	2
Bench, c	3	2	1	0	8	1
Perez, 1b	3	2	2	4	5	0
Foster, lf	4	0	0	0	2	0
Concepcion, ss	2	0	0	1	0	0
Geronimo, cf	4	0	0	0	6	0
Gullett, p	3	1	1	0	0	0
Eastwick, p	0	0	0	0	0	0
Totals	29	6	8	6	27	3

```
Boston      ......... 1 0 0  0 0 0  0 0 1—2
Cincinnati  ......... 0 0 0  1 1 3  0 1 x—6
```

Boston	IP.	H.	R.	ER.	BB.	SO.
Cleveland (L)	5*	7	5	5	2	3
Willoughby	2	1	0	0	0	1
Pole	0†	0	1	1	2	0
Segui	1	0	0	0	0	0

Cincinnati	IP.	H.	R.	ER.	BB.	SO.
Gullett (W)	8⅔	5	2	2	1	7
Eastwick (S)	⅓	0	0	0	0	1

Game 7

Wednesday, October 22, At Boston

Cincinnati	AB.	R.	H.	RBI.	PO.	A.
Rose, 3b	4	0	2	1	2	2
Morgan, 2b	4	0	2	1	2	4
Bench, c	4	1	0	0	7	0
Perez, 1b	5	1	1	2	8	1
Foster, lf	4	0	1	0	1	0
Concepcion, ss	4	2	1	0	0	2
Griffey, rf	3	0	0	0	3	0
Geronimo, cf	1	0	1	0	0	0
Gullett, p	1	0	0	0	0	0
aRettenmund	1	0	0	0	0	0
Billingham, p	0	0	0	0	0	0
bArmbrister	0	0	0	0	1	0
Carroll, p	1	0	0	0	0	0
dDriessen	0	0	0	0	0	0
McEnaney, p	0	0	0	0	0	0
Totals	33	4	9	4	27	9

Boston	AB.	R.	H.	RBI.	PO.	A.
Carbo, lf	3	1	1	0	0	1
Miller, lf	0	0	0	0	0	0
eBeniquez	1	0	0	0	0	0
Doyle, 2b	4	1	1	0	5	3
fMontgomery	1	0	0	0	0	0
Yastrzemski, 1b	5	1	1	1	9	0
Fisk, c	3	0	0	0	4	0
Lynn, cf	2	0	0	0	1	0
Petrocelli, 3b	3	0	1	1	1	3
Evans, rf	2	0	0	1	5	0
Burleson, ss	3	0	1	0	0	1
Lee, p	3	0	0	0	0	0
Moret, p	0	0	0	0	0	0
Willoughby, p	0	0	0	0	0	0
cCooper	1	0	0	0	0	0
Burton, p	0	0	0	0	0	0
Cleveland, p	0	0	0	0	0	0
Totals	31	3	5	3	27	15

```
Cincinnati  ......... 0 0 0  0 0 2  1 0 1—4
Boston      ......... 0 0 3  0 0 0  0 0 0—3
```

Cincinnati	IP.	H.	R.	ER.	BB.	SO.
Gullett	4	4	3	3	5	5
Billingham	2	1	0	0	2	1
Carroll (W)	2	0	0	0	1	1
McEnaney (S)	1	0	0	0	0	1

Boston	IP.	H.	R.	ER.	BB.	SO.
Lee	6⅓	7	3	3	1	2
Moret	⅓	1	0	0	2	0
Willoughby	1⅓	0	0	0	0	0
Burton (L)	⅔	1	1	1	2	0
Cleveland	⅓	0	0	0	1	0

Game 6

Tuesday, October 21, At Boston

Cincinnati	AB.	R.	H.	RBI.	PO.	A.
Rose, 3b	5	1	2	0	0	2
Griffey, rf	5	2	2	0	4	4
Morgan, 2b	6	1	1	0	4	4
Bench, c	6	0	1	1	8	0
Perez, 1b	6	0	2	0	11	2
Foster, lf	6	0	2	2	4	1
Concepcion, ss	6	0	1	0	3	4
Geronimo, cf	6	1	2	1	2	0
Nolan, p	1	0	0	0	1	0
aChaney	1	0	0	0	0	0
Norman, p	0	0	0	0	0	0
Billingham, p	0	0	0	0	0	0
bArmbrister	0	1	0	0	0	0
Carroll, p	0	0	0	0	0	0
cCrowley	1	0	1	0	0	0
Borbon, p	1	0	0	0	0	0
Eastwick, p	0	0	0	0	0	0
McEnaney, p	0	0	0	0	0	0
eDriessen	1	0	0	0	0	0
Darcy, p	0	0	0	0	0	0
Totals	50	6	14	6	33	14

Boston	AB.	R.	H.	RBI.	PO.	A.
Cooper, 1b	5	0	0	0	8	0
Drago, p	0	0	0	0	0	0
fMiller	1	0	0	0	0	0
Wise, p	0	0	0	0	0	0
Doyle, 2b	5	0	1	0	2	0
Yastrzemski, lf-1b	6	1	3	0	7	1
Fisk, c	4	2	2	1	9	1
Lynn, cf	4	2	2	3	2	0
Petrocelli, 3b	4	1	0	0	1	1
Evans, rf	5	0	1	0	5	1
Burleson, ss	3	0	0	0	3	2
Tiant, p	2	0	0	0	0	2
Moret, p	0	0	0	0	0	1
dCarbo, lf	2	1	1	3	1	0
Totals	41	7	10	7	36	11

```
Cincinnati  ...... 0 0 0  0 3 0  2 1 0  0 0 0—6
Boston      ...... 3 0 0  0 0 0  0 3 0  0 0 1—7
```

None out when winning run scored.

Cincinnati	IP.	H.	R.	ER.	BB.	SO.
Nolan	2	3	3	3	0	2
Norman	⅔	1	0	0	2	0
Billingham	1⅓	1	0	0	1	1
Carroll	1	0	0	0	0	0
Borbon	2†	1	2	2	1	1
Eastwick	1⅓	2	1	1	1	2
McEnaney	1	0	0	0	1	0
Darcy (L)	2⅓	1	1	1	0	1

Boston	IP.	H.	R.	ER.	BB.	SO.
Tiant	7*	11	6	6	2	5
Moret	1	0	0	0	0	0
Drago	3	1	0	0	0	1
Wise (W)	1	2	0	0	0	1

CHAPTER

5

1991

Atlanta Braves

vs.

Minnesota Twins

From Worst to First

After his superhuman performance in Game 7, Twins pitcher Jack Morris celebrated on his pickup truck while he was driven through the streets of Minneapolis. Morris was named the Most Valuable Player of the World Series. (AP/Wide World Photos)

wins take Series o the 7th game with close victory

Morris goes seve for victor

By Dick Polman
Inquirer Staff Writer

WORLD SERIES, from 1-E

ats with runners in scoring posi-
. By contrast, the Braves had hit
at the Chop Shop and had
gged the overburdened Minne-
a bullpen.

Braves finally caught up with him.

With one out and a runner aboard,
Pendleton was served a belt-high
pitch on the inside half of the plate.
He hammered the ball to the folded
seats behind the center field wall

MINNEAPOLIS — Game 1 of the
World Series, a frenzied affair
niscent of being chained to a
speaker at a Van Halen concer
tured Minnesota Twins baseball
Mark Guthrie. Kelly, wh
in the week joked that h
and turned endlessly ir
challenge of managing
designated hitter, migl
lost sleep Tuesday nig
verings had se
different players
us strand himself
bench in the 1
ut to center.

Tenth inning. No score. Bases loaded. After seven gut-wrenching games, the World Championship came down to this pitch. Alejandro Pena let fly and Gene Larkin took a rip. The rest is history. (AP/Wide World Photos)

m of the 12th

id Justice, whos
et fully sweet, is
been lately, line
off Aguilera and
then walked, an
ng to the plate, hi
a distant memo
single to score J
al memento.

na had an innin
erish, but that he
ena, who had re
4 chances with th
three against the
nal League Cham
ve up a two-ru
run to Chili Davi
l to mist.

g toward greate
inning unfolded
and Kent Hrbe
it to put Twins a
the possibly decic
m the plate. Bu

The Last Shall Be First

A happy blend of whiz kids and free agents help Minnesota and Atlanta vault from the cellar to the World Series

By RICHARD CORLISS

They picked Cinderella for last place
too, and she did all right. But even in a
fairy tale, no one expects Prince Charming
to be that ungainly lad who'd been kept in
the cellar for the past three years.

The improbable is for fables; baseball,
right now at least, is the art of the impossible. In a century of the sport, no team had
vaulted in a single year from worst in its
league to best. Last week two teams did.
And over the w

Pittsburgh Pirates, with a core of fine
young stars, got that now-or-never feeling
this year. Why? Because slugger Bobby
Bonilla is expected to become a zillionaire
elsewhere this winter, and Most Valuable
Player candidate Barry Bonds may walk
next October. Pittsburgh, in a modest TV
market, certainly can't afford them both.
So the bucks—and the Bucs—stop here.

In baseball, as in other businesses, two
cardinal rules apply: be smart and be lucky.
The postmodern era adds: but first you must

*W*hen something really bad happens, you know what it feels like. You feel terrible. You feel like it's the end of the world. You feel like you'll never be able to feel good about yourself again. You feel like giving up.

Well, this chapter proves that it's possible to bounce back from the worst possible circumstances and come out on top of the world.

Since the modern World Series began in 1903, no team had ever gone from last place one season to first place the next season. But in 1991, two teams did.

In 1990, the Atlanta Braves lost 97 games and the Minnesota Twins lost 88. Each finished dead last in its division.* The next season, both of these teams picked up a few free agents, made good trades, brought up hot rookies and got great performances from ordinary players. Everything came together. The Twins won 21 more games than they had the previous year, and the Braves won 29 more games.

Incredibly, two of the worst teams of 1990 became the two best teams of 1991. Together they would duke it out in the World Series.

And what a Series it was! Five of the seven games were decided by one run. Three games went into extra innings. Four games were up in the air until the final pitch. That spells edge-of-your-seat baseball.

"Let us call this Series what it is," wrote *Sports Illus-*

*In fact, the Braves had been cellar-dwellers three years in a row.

trated when it was all over, "the greatest that was ever played."

The players who participated in this great Series, for the most part, were not a bunch of high-priced superstars. The Braves' strongest assets were their sharp, young starting pitchers: Tom Glavine (20–11), Steve Avery (18–8), and John Smoltz (14–13). Between them, they threw three shutouts in the National League playoffs. All three of them were barely old enough to vote.

Centerfielder Ron Gant slugged 32 home runs. Right-fielder David Justice, in his second season, chipped in 21 more. Third baseman Terry "TP" Pendleton had his best year ever, hitting .319 with 22 home runs. The rest of the infield was filled with a bunch of no-names—Sid Bream (.253) at first, little Mark Lemke (.234) at second, Rafael Belliard (.249) at short, and Greg Olson (.241) behind the plate.

But the Braves, led by first-time manager Bobby Cox, also had a *secret* weapon. Leftfielder Lonnie Smith was the only man in baseball history to play in four different World Series with four different teams. Smith came up to the big leagues with the Phillies in 1980 and they won the pennant. He was with the Cardinals in 1982 and they won the pennant. In 1985, he played for the Kansas City Royals and *they* won the pennant. All three times, Smith's team went on to win the World Series.

Now Lonnie Smith was playing for Atlanta, and—

naturally—they won the pennant. Knowing that Smith was in the dugout, with his three World Series rings, had to give the Braves a little extra confidence.

The Minnesota Twins (sometimes called Twinderella) were no strangers to the World Series. They won it in 1987. Their leader then, and their leader this time, was centerfielder Kirby Puckett. Puckett got four hits in his first big league game in 1984 and never looked back. At five-foot-eight with a body like a fire hydrant, Kirby hit .319 with 15 homers and 89 RBIs. He was known for coming through in the clutch, and was the Most Valuable Player of the American League playoffs.

Puckett was surrounded by rightfielder Shane Mack (.310, 18 homers) and leftfielder Dan Gladden (.247). The Twin infield was patrolled by Kent Hrbek (.284, 20 homers) at first, Rookie of the Year second baseman Chuck Knoblauch (.281), and shortstop Greg Gagne (.265). Platooned at third base were lefthander Mike Pagliarulo (.279) and righthander Scott Leius (.286).

Catcher Brian Harper had bounced around with eight minor league teams and was ready to give up baseball in 1987. His wife, Chris, encouraged him to stick it out, and he was signed by Minnesota. Harper would go on to hit .295 in 1988, .325 in 1989, .294 in 1990, and .311 in 1991—another castoff who went from worst to first.

Minnesota's pitchers were nothing to sneeze at either. Their opponents learned not to expect many high-scoring games, knowing they had to face veteran Jack Morris

(18–12), Scott Erickson (20–8), Kevin Tapani (16–9), and Rick Aguilera (42 saves).

GAME 1. The Hubert H. Humphrey Metrodome in Minneapolis is sometimes called the Decibel Dome because it's so loud. The sound of the crowd cheering has nowhere to escape. Instead of shouting, "I got it!" outfielders sometimes communicate with each other by waving their arms. In the stands, you have to cup your hands to talk with the person sitting next to you. In the bullpen, a coach sits with his foot on the telephone. He can't hear it ring, but he can feel the vibrations. One fan held a banner that read, FEEL THE THUNDER.

The noise in the dome has been clocked at 125 decibels. By comparison, a jet taking off is 120 decibels.

Minnesota fans don't just cheer rallies, they start them. When 50,000 people begin screaming and waving their "homer hankies," opposing teams want to crawl under the artificial turf and hide.

The Twins won all four games played in the Metrodome during the 1987 World Series. A sign outside the Twin clubhouse said, TAKE US BACK TO BASEBALL HEAVEN, JUST LIKE YOU DID IN '87.

The first ball was thrown out by umpire Steve Palermo. Earlier in the season, Palermo had been shot trying to prevent a robbery outside a restaurant in Dallas. He was paralyzed and didn't take a step for three months. As Palermo bravely walked to the pitcher's mound with the aid of crutches, fans realized they were witnessing a worst-to-first story that was more inspiring than any baseball team.

Jack Morris, who was born in St. Paul, Minnesota, would start the Series for the Twins. Morris was a guy who knew how to win. He had already piled up 216 career victories, winning 20 games two seasons, 19 once, 18 twice, 17 twice, 16 twice, and 15 twice. That's consistency. Coming off two victories in the American League play-offs, Morris was at the top of his game. He needed just 40 pitches to blank the Braves in the first three innings.

Instead of starting one of their young phenoms, Atlanta elected to open the Series with a more experienced pitcher—35-year-old lefthander Charlie Leibrandt. He had pitched six years for Kansas City, so he knew the American League. Leibrandt was a master of the change-up and used it to win 15 games during the regular season. He had a 17–9 year in 1985.

The Twins went down quietly in the first two innings. In the third, Leibrandt walked Twins leftfielder Dan Gladden. Gladden stole second and scored the first run of the World Series on a single by 23-year-old second baseman Chuck Knoblauch. Twins 1, Braves 0. The noise inside the Metrodome was deafening, but it was nothing to what it sounded like in the fifth inning.

Kent Hrbek led off for the Twins. Another Minnesota boy, Hrbek was born right there in Minneapolis. When the Metrodome opened in 1982, it was Herby who hit the first home run there.

Leibrandt served up a fat pitch and Hrbek whaled a double off the "Glad Bag"—the black, padded rightfield wall. Scott Leius followed with a single to left, moving Hrbek to third.

The number-nine hitter, shortstop Greg Gagne, was up. Leibrandt tried to jam him, but he missed the inside corner and the ball was over the heart of the plate. Gagne, who hit eight homers all year, cranked a blast that carried well over the Plexiglas wall in leftfield. The three Twins crossed the plate and Minnesota was ahead, 4–0.

The stadium was a sea of homer hankies. From the sound of the crowd, you would think World War II had just ended.

The Braves picked up a run off Jack Morris in the sixth inning to make it 4–1, but the Twins came right back in their half when Kent Hrbek creamed a shot over the wall, over the seats behind the wall, over two outfield press boxes, and over the scoreboard.

Jack Morris held the Braves to five hits through seven innings. Rick Aguilera relieved him in the eighth and finished things off. The final score was Twins 5, Braves 2. It would be back to the Metrodome the next day for Game 2.

GAME 2. The two starting pitchers for the second game of the Series continued the worst-to-first story.

Tom Glavine was a schoolboy hockey star in Massachusetts, and he was drafted by the Los Angeles Kings in 1984. He chose to become a baseball pitcher instead.

It didn't seem like a smart move for the left-hander in the beginning. As a rookie for Atlanta in 1988, Glavine led the league in losses, posting a dismal 7–17 record. But Glavine came back the next year to go 14–8. In 1991, he won 20 games and the Cy Young Award.

Kevin Tapani, the Twins starter, was an unlikely success story, too. Less than two years earlier, Tapani was working part time as a Federal Express delivery man to supplement his skimpy minor league salary. He started the 1991 season with six straight losses, but went 11–2 after the All-Star break.

Now these two pitchers would be starting Game 2 of the World Series.

Tapani retired the Braves 1–2–3 in the first inning, but Glavine got into trouble. The first Twins hitter, Dan Gladden, hit a fly ball to shallow right-field. It was catchable, but the ceiling of the Metrodome is white, and outfielders often have trouble following the ball up there. Atlanta rightfielder David Justice rushed in and second baseman Mark Lemke backpedaled. Just as the ball hit Lemke's glove, he collided with Justice and the ball popped out. Gladden was safe at second.

Glavine walked Chuck Knoblauch, putting runners at first and second with nobody out. The always-dangerous

Kirby Puckett was up. PUCKETT WILL PARK IT! predicted a banner in the stands.

Puckett slapped a broken bat grounder toward third base. The head of the bat flew to third, too. Terry Pendleton grabbed the ball, avoided the bat, stepped on third and fired to first to complete the double play. Knoblauch was safe at second, but there were two outs.

Chili Davis, the Twins designated hitter, was up. Chili Davis's real name is Charles Theodore Davis. He was nicknamed Chili as a boy in Jamaica after receiving a particularly bad haircut that was shaped from a chili bowl put on his head.

Anyway, it didn't seem to hurt his hitting. Chili Davis hit 20 or more home runs five seasons, culminating in a career high of 29 dingers in 1991.

Make that 30. With an 0–1 count, Glavine threw a slider down and in. Davis nailed it over the wall in left centerfield. Chuck Knoblauch crossed the plate in front of Chili, and the Twins had a 2–0 first-inning lead.

After that, Glavine settled down. The Braves scored a run in the second inning and another in the fifth, both on sacrifice flies. The game was tied at 2–2.

There was a weird play in the Atlanta half of the third inning. Lonnie Smith was the runner at first base with two outs when Ron Gant singled. Smith advanced to third. Gant made the big turn at first, and then scampered back to the bag as the throw came in to Twins first baseman Kent Hrbek.

Hrbek weighed 253 pounds and had stated in interviews that after his baseball career he planned to become a professional wrestler using the name T-Rex. When Gant (192 pounds) ran back to first, Hrbek grabbed him by the leg as he tagged him. Gant fell off the base in Hrbek's arms. The umpire called Gant out. Hrbek's wrestling career was off to a good start.

Wrestlemania. Minnesota first baseman Kent Hrbek "gently" shoves Ron Gant off the bag after Gant scampered back to first base. Hrbek got the call. (AP/Wide World Photos)

Ron Gant was furious, kicking over water buckets in the Atlanta dugout. But the umpire's decision stood, and the inning was over. Hrbek's tag would become a key play, because this would turn out to be a one-run game, and who knows what might have happened if the Braves had been able to keep hitting with runners at first and third?

Glavine and Tapani were both pitching a great game and the score remained tied at 2–2 into the eighth inning. Glavine was working on a two-hitter, and at one stretch he retired 15 Twins in a row.

Rookie third baseman Scott Leius led off the bottom of the eighth for the Twins. Leius was looking for his first postseason hit.

He didn't have to look for long. The first pitch from Glavine was over the plate and Leius jumped all over it. The ball sailed off to leftfield. Brian Hunter dashed back, looking up, and kept running back until he ran out of room. As he bumped into the Plexiglas wall, the ball landed in a sea of waving homer hankies.

Twins 3, Braves 2. As Leius enjoyed the seventh home run trot of his career, the Metrodome shook with noise.

Terry Pendleton dives into first after hitting a slow roller in the eighth inning. Twins pitcher Kevin Tapani (36) tried to make the play, but Pendleton was safe. (AP/Wide World Photos)

For the second game in a row, the bottom of the Twins batting order had come through.

That would do it for Game 2. Rick Aguilera came in to strike out the side in the ninth. Tom Glavine had pitched a complete game for the Braves, but he took the loss. Kevin Tapani was winning pitcher. Not bad for a Federal Express delivery man.

Now Atlanta was down by two games and grateful to get out of the Metrodome with their eardrums intact. The Braves hitters were ice cold. They hadn't hit a home run in the first two games, while the Twins slugged four.

"Has the bubble burst for Atlanta?" asked CBS announcer Jack Buck. "We'll find out starting Tuesday."

GAME 3.   The banner outside Atlanta's Fulton County Stadium read, THE BRAVES—TOO LEGIT TO QUIT. This was a must-win game for the Braves. If they lost it, they'd be down by three games. The Braves had gone from worst to first, but it might be asking too much for them to lose the first three games of the World Series and come back to win it. No team in baseball history has ever accomplished that.

The city of Atlanta was Indian-crazy all season. When the Braves started winning, a savvy Georgian named Paul Braddy quit his job and borrowed $5,000 to make foam rubber tomahawks. He quickly sold 200,000 of them. Soon, Atlanta games were a combination of baseball, synchronized tomahawk chopping, and droning Indian war chants. Even former President Jimmy Carter, a Georgia native, became caught up in the Chop.

Outside the ballpark, the American Indian Movement was picketing. In their view, tomahawk chopping and sports nicknames like Braves, Indians, and Redskins are disrespectful to Native Americans.

Jimmy Carter believed otherwise: "With the Braves on top, we have a brave, courageous, and successful team, and I think we can look on the American Indians as brave, successful, and attractive. So I don't look on it as an insult." But the Indians got their message out, and the World Series went on.

The Braves were two games down and had their backs against the wall, but they had a few things going for them now. They were playing in front of their hometown fans, for one thing. Also, in National League parks designated hitters are not used, so the Twins starting lineup would be without the potent bat of Chili Davis.

Most important, Atlanta's "young guns"—Steve Avery and John Smoltz—would be pitching the next two games. During the National League playoff, these two had a combined earned run average of 0.85. In other words, they held their opponent to *less than one* run a game.

BRAVES WIN AVERY TIME, read a banner in the rightfield stands. Avery was simply amazing. Just 21 years old, the lefty had an 18–8 season and tossed two 1–0 shutouts in the playoffs. Steve's father, Ken Avery, had been a good minor-league pitcher. He quit baseball when the Detroit

Tigers organization refused to increase his salary to $800 a month.

As a boy, Steve was small and frail, with little arm strength. To compensate, he learned to snap off curveballs that turned batters into statues. As he grew up, Steve's fastball developed. Now he could crank it up to 98 miles an hour. Despite his age, Avery was so relaxed that he'd sometimes take a nap on the trainer's table before pitching.

With all the hoopla over Avery, it was easy to overlook the Twins starter, 23-year-old Scott Erickson. Nicknamed Superman because he resembled actor Christopher Reeve, Erickson won 12 games in a row during the regular season and finished with a 20–8 record. Erickson didn't take naps before pitching. He called his mother to hear her say, "Good luck."

There was a big, full moon in the sky over Fulton County Stadium. This would be the first World Series ever played in this ballpark. The town wanted to win badly—Atlanta had never won a World Championship in baseball, football, basketball, or hockey.

The first ball was thrown out by Hank Aaron, who hit his historic 715th home run here in 1974 to break Babe Ruth's career record.

Steve Avery was feeling some jitters as he took the mound to start the game. Dan Gladden sliced his third pitch to right for a triple. Chuck Knoblauch's sacrifice fly brought the run in and it was Twins 1, Braves 0.

The crowd, which had been chopping and chanting enthusiastically, suddenly became quiet. This could be a long night for Atlanta.

But the Braves came right back to tie it in the second inning with a walk and two singles. Twins 1, Braves 1.

After giving up the first-inning run, Steve Avery regained his composure and began pitching the way he knew how. He struck out the next three hitters, and began mowing down Twins. By the third inning, he had struck out five of them. He retired 15 batters in a row. He was looking unhittable.

On the other side, Scott Erickson was shaky. His fastball was clocking about five miles an hour slower than usual. In the fourth inning, he threw a 3–1 pitch that David Justice deposited over the rightfield wall for Atlanta's first homer of the Series. The next inning, Erickson threw Lonnie Smith an eye-high change-up that Smith slammed into the leftfield seats. At the end of five innings, Atlanta had a 4–1 lead and Erickson had hit the showers.

But the Minnesota Twins didn't reach the World Series by giving up when they were behind. Kirby Puckett, who hadn't yet made a hit in the World Series, crushed Steve Avery's second pitch of the seventh inning for a homer over the leftfield wall. That made it Braves 4, Twins 2.

Avery appeared to be tiring, and in the eighth inning Alejandro Pena relieved him. Since coming over from the Mets in mid-season, Pena had been perfect—14 saves in 14 save opportunities. The man just did not blow a lead.

If Pena could get six outs, the Braves would win the game and they'd be back in the Series.

Brian Harper reached on an error, and it was the pitcher's turn to bat. It came as no surprise when Chili Davis stepped out of the Twins dugout to pinch hit. Davis, who hit a homer in Game 2, had been benched because designated hitters were not used in National League parks.

Alejandro Pena glanced at the runner on first and threw a fastball to Davis. Chili connected and sent a bullet to left. Amazingly, for the second game in a row, Chili Davis hit a two-run homer. With time running out, the Twins had tied it: 4–4.

It was desperation time for Atlanta. They couldn't afford to lose this game. The Twins, revived, began to smell victory. Both teams would pull out all the stops in an attempt to score the next run or prevent their opponent from scoring it.

In the bottom of the ninth, the Braves had the winning run at second base with one out. They couldn't bring it home.

In the top of the tenth, the Twins had the winning run at second with one out. They couldn't score either.

In the bottom of the tenth, the Braves got the winning run to second again with two outs. Once again, it died there.

Neither team scored in the eleventh inning. Tension was mounting. Both teams were exhausting their supply of pinch hitters and relief pitchers. The box score of this game lists 42 players, which is a World Series record.

With one out in the Twins half of the twelfth, Dan Gladden slashed a single to right off Mark Wohlers. Chuck Knoblauch was up next. He slapped a sharp grounder to the right side. Second baseman Mark Lemke wanted a double play badly, but he broke a rule every Little Leaguer learns—*Don't try to make the throw until you have the ball in your hand.* Lemke took his eye off the grounder for an instant and it scooted through his legs.

The Twins had runners at first and third. The go-ahead run was 90 feet from the plate. Kent Hrbek was coming up with the chance to be the hero.

"Cheater! Cheater! Cheater!" chanted the Atlanta fans. They were referring to the play in Game 2 when Hrbek wrestled Ron Gant off first base to tag him. Somebody in the stands held a sign that read, HRBEK—BUY A VOWEL!

Another left-handed Kent, Kent Mercker, was brought in to face Kent Hrbek. He struck him out for the second out of the inning.

That brought up Kirby Puckett, who had already hit a home run in the game. With the winning run at third, there was no way Atlanta was going to pitch to Puckett. He was walked intentionally to load the bases.

It was the pitcher's turn to bat. Twins' relief pitcher Mark Guthrie had the chance to win his own game. There was just one problem—in his entire professional baseball career, Mark Guthrie had never stepped into a batter's box.

Twins manager Tom Kelly looked up and down his

dugout. He had already used seven pinch hitters. There wasn't a left- or right-handed batter on the team who hadn't already been in the game. He had no hitters left.

Then Kelly had an idea. Relief pitcher Rick Aguilera started out as a shortstop and had been a pretty good-hitting pitcher back when he played for the Mets in the National League (.203 average, three homers). It had been 25 years since a pitcher pinch hit in the World Series,* but Kelly had no other choice. Aguilera grabbed a bat and settled into the batter's box.

Dan Gladden danced up and down the line at third. If Aguilera could get a hit, a walk, or even manage to get hit by a pitch, Gladden would score and put the Twins on top.

The pitch came in and Aguilera hit it solidly. It was a line drive to leftfield. Ron Gant dashed over.

Out! The game was still tied. 50,878 Braves fans exhaled.

Rick Aguilera stayed in the game in the bottom of the twelfth. He was the seventh Twins pitcher, and the last one left in the bullpen. That meant he would have to stay on the mound no matter how many innings the game went. It was Aguilera's game to win or lose.

Game 3 was into its fourth hour now. In the Atlanta dugout, catcher Greg Olson was sitting next to second baseman Mark Lemke.

"You're gonna get the game-winning hit, Lumpy," Olson said.

*That was Don Drysdale, in 1965.

"Ehhh, I don't think so," Lemke replied. He was still upset about the error he made at the top of the inning that almost cost Atlanta the game.

Ron Gant led off with a fly ball to centerfield. One out. David Justice lined a single to right. Brian Hunter popped up to second base. Two outs. While Greg Olson was up, Justice stole second. Again Atlanta had the winning run in scoring position. The Minnesota outfield moved in to choke off a run at the plate. Aguilera walked Olson.

Runners at first and second. Two outs. Bottom of the twelfth. Mark Lemke was up with the chance to win it right here. He was a switch hitter, batting left-handed.

Lemke took ball one, and then a strike. Aguilera's next delivery was a fastball on the outside part of the plate. Lemke went with the pitch, and the ball shot over the shortstop's head for a single.

Justice took off from second base.

Dan Gladden got to the ball quickly in leftfield.

Justice got the green light to try for home. He rounded third.

Gladden wound up for his throw to the plate. Catcher Brian Harper got himself ready to receive it and slap the tag on Justice.

Justice charged for the plate.

The ball bounced twice. Harper grabbed it.

Justice slid to the left of the plate and reached out with his right hand to touch home as he slid by.

Harper dove for Justice's hand.

Safe!

The marathon game was over, and the Braves had won, 5–4. Brian Harper lay in the dirt while Atlanta erupted in celebration. They were behind two games to one, but they were back in the Series.

Afterwards, somebody asked Twins manager Tom Kelly if he would do anything differently.

"Replay the game," Kelly replied.

GAME 4.   Finally, John Smoltz, another worst-to-first story, got a turn. Smoltz started the season with just two wins against 11 defeats for Atlanta. He made a slight adjustment in his delivery, and through the rest of the season won 14 games while losing only two.

Smoltz grew up in Detroit. When he was a boy, he went to Tiger Stadium to watch Jack Morris pitch for the Tigers. Now 24, John Smoltz was facing Morris (36 years old) in the World Series.

Both pitchers did their jobs in the first inning. In the Twins half of the second, Brian Harper led off with a shot to rightfield. David Justice dove for it, but the ball ticked off the end of his glove. Harper was safe at second. He scored on a single by Mike Pagliarulo. Twins 1, Braves 0.

Atlanta came right back in the third when Terry Pendleton took a 3–1 fastball from Morris and drove it over the rightfield wall. Twins 1, Braves 1.

The fourth inning was uneventful, but the bottom of the fifth was a wild one. Lonnie Smith started things off with a single to left. Smith stole second while Terry Pendleton was up, and then Pendleton smashed a line drive to centerfield over Kirby Puckett's head.

The ball hit the wall on a bounce. Puckett played the carom cleanly and whipped the ball to Chuck Knoblauch for the relay throw.

Lonnie Smith was chugging home. His helmet had flown off his head, and his gold chain was flapping with each stride.

Knoblauch's throw to the plate was on the money. Smith knew he was a dead duck. His only hope was to jar the ball loose from catcher Brian Harper.

In his baseball career, Harper had been released by three major-league teams. He was a good hitter, but the word had gotten around that he was a lousy catcher.

Lonnie Smith knew he was a dead duck at the plate. His only hope was to jar the ball loose from Minnesota catcher Brian Harper. It was a spectacular collision, but when both men got up off the dirt, Harper held the ball. (AP/Wide World Photos)

Harper gloved the ball on a short hop and blocked the plate. Smith put his forearms in front of his chest and rammed into the catcher. Harper tumbled backward and the two of them crashed to the dirt.

The ball was still in Harper's hand. Out!

"That's the greatest collision I've ever seen," said announcer Jack Buck. "I don't know how Harper held onto the ball," added Buck's partner Tim McCarver.

Terry Pendleton made it to third in all the commotion. Moments later, Pendleton tried to score on a wild pitch. Harper, still dazed from the collision with Lonnie Smith, grabbed the loose ball and dove for the sliding Pendleton. Out!

For a lousy catcher, Brian Harper was having a great inning. By the time it was over, there had been a single, a double, a walk, a stolen base, and a wild pitch. But because of Brian Harper's roadblock defense, the Braves didn't get a run across the plate. The score remained tied at 1–1 through six innings.

That became 2–2 in the seventh inning. Mike Pagliarulo hit a solo homer to right for the Twins, and Lonnie Smith countered with a tremendous blast to straightaway centerfield for the Braves. Smith's homer was his second in two days.

John Smoltz and Jack Morris both pitched a good game, but neither would be involved in the final decision. By the eighth inning, each had been lifted for a pinch hitter.

Going into the bottom of the ninth with the score still tied, Atlanta fans began chopping and chanting. They wanted a run now. So did the Braves. In the dugout, the entire team put their caps on upside-down for luck. They called this their shark rally cap—because the Braves were going for the kill.

Greg Olson grounded to short for the first out. That brought up Mark Lemke. The hero from the night before had already hit a single and a double, and was quickly becoming the darling of Atlanta. His teammates called him Dirt because he played so hard.

Right-hander Mark Guthrie was on the mound in relief for the Twins, so Lemke was hitting from the left side. Guthrie's first pitch looked juicy, and Lemke nailed it. The ball sailed off to left and didn't come down until it hit the base of the wall. Leftfielder Dan Gladden bobbled it briefly. By the time he got it in, Lemke was on third and Atlanta Fulton County Stadium sounded like the Battle of Little Big Horn.

Tie game. Bottom of the ninth. The winning run was on third. One out. A fly ball could win it for the Braves. The Twins outfield moved in.

It was light-hitting shortstop Rafael Belliard's turn to hit, but Atlanta manager Bobby Cox wanted someone up there who could drive the ball far. Jerry Willard stepped out of the dugout and approached the plate.

Jerry who? Willard was a journeyman catcher who spent most of his career in the minors, playing for nearly a dozen different teams. He had been to bat only 14 times all season, and just 3 times the season before. Usually, Willard's biggest responsibility was to squat in the bullpen and warm up relief pitchers. Now his job was to win the game and tie the World Series for Atlanta.

The Twins brought in Steve Bedrosian to pitch to Willard. Bedrock, as he was called, had won the Cy Young Award in 1987. He got a ball and two strikes on Willard. The next pitch was close enough to the strike zone that the umpire might call it a strike. Willard had to swing to protect the plate. He made contact, a fly ball to medium rightfield.

Rightfielder Shane Mack had a good arm. Mark Lemke, ready to tag up at third, knew it.

Mack backed up a few steps and caught the ball.

Lemke took off for home.

Mack's throw was true. It arrived at the plate about the same time as Lemke.

Lemke realized that if Lonnie Smith (170 pounds) hadn't been able to jar a ball loose from Harper (195 pounds) in the fifth inning, then he (167 pounds) certainly wouldn't be able to either. Instead, Lemke slid around Harper, much like David Justice did scoring the game-winning run the night before.

Lemke swiped at the plate with his left hand as he slid by. Harper lunged at Lemke with his glove.

"Ouuuu—Safe! Safe! Safe!" shouted Jack Buck. "They called him safe!"

"No way!" screamed Brian Harper, jumping up and down in front of the umpire. "No way! I got him!" Harper threw down his mask and mitt in disgust.

But that didn't change the fact that the game was over, and the Braves had won it by the score of 3–2. The World Series was all tied up at two games apiece.

For the second night in a row, Mark Lemke was the hero. If he had run for mayor of Atlanta, it would have been no contest.

GAME 5. After two heart-stopping games in which the winning run scored on the final pitch, everybody was somewhat relieved that Game 5 wasn't so nerve-racking.

Everybody on the Atlanta Braves, anyway. The Braves demolished the Twins by the score of 14–5. It would be the only blowout of this World Series.

Because of the lopsided score, Game 5 wasn't all that exciting. But here are a few statistics . . .

The Braves banged out 17 hits, and everybody contributed. Ron Gant and Greg Olson each had three. Lonnie Smith hit a homer for the third day in a row. Mark Lemke drove in three runs with two triples. David Justice hit a homer and drove in five runs. Brian Hunter had two hits, one of them a tremendous two-run homer. Terry Pendleton had two hits. Rafael Belliard drove in a run.

By the seventh inning, the Braves rooters were chanting, WE WILL WE WILL ROCK YOU! and the Twins just wanted to get the humiliation over with.

The Braves had swept the three games in Atlanta. Now they were ahead in the World Series, three games to two. The Minnesota Twins were one game away from a long winter.

GAME 6. As the players returned to Minnesota for Game 6, the Twins were grim. Scott Erickson, who would start the game, had been banged around by Atlanta in Game 3. This would be the first time in his career that he'd pitched with only three days of rest.

The Twins hitters had averaged just .218 in the World Series so far. Kirby Puckett had just three hits and one RBI in 18 at-bats. Kent Hrbek was 3 for 19. Shane Mack had been up 15 times, but had yet to get a hit.

To make things worse, they would be batting against the unflappable Steve Avery. If the kid won Game 6, he'd be on every Wheaties box for the next ten years. Things looked good for the Braves to finish the Twins off.

But Atlanta would have to win in the Metrodome— where the Twins had never been defeated in a World Series game. With all the crowd noise and the waving homer hankies, there was a definite "dome-field" advantage.

With one out in the Twins half of the first inning, Chuck Knoblauch singled hard to rightfield. Kirby Puckett was up. He banged Avery's second pitch on the ground down the third-base line. It was fair by about a foot and bounded into the leftfield corner. Brian Hunter got set to play the carom off the wall, but the ball bounced off a pole and took a crazy hop. By the time he threw the ball in, Knoblauch had scored and Puckett was standing on third base. Twins 1, Braves 0.

The crowd in the Metrodome was screaing its head off. The noise became almost unbearable when Shane Mack rapped a broken bat single to left to score Puckett. Twins 2, Braves 0.

THE CHOP IS A FLOP! somebody's banner said.

Once Avery made it through the first inning, he found his rhythm and was firing his fastball in the 95-mile-an-hour range. The Braves were hitting Scott Erickson's pitches hard, but usually right at somebody. Erickson blanked the Braves through four innings, allowing just two hits.

In the Braves half of the fifth, Rafael Belliard led off with a single to left. Lonnie Smith grounded into a force play, but Terry Pendleton took one look at Erickson's first pitch—a belt-high fastball on the inside corner—and hammered it over the centerfield fence. It was the second homer of the Series for Pendleton, and it tied the game at 2–2.

In the bottom half of that inning, the Twins pulled ahead again on a walk, a stolen base, and two sacrifice flies. Twins 3, Braves 2.

The amazing Mark Lemke started off the seventh inning for the Braves with a single. It was his ninth hit of the Series, bringing his batting average up to .474. That knocked Scott Erickson out of the box. Mark Guthrie was brought in to relieve him.

Lemke advanced to second base on a Guthrie wild pitch. Runner on second, nobody out. The Braves had a golden opportunity to score the tying run. Guthrie struck out pinch hitter Jeff Blauser for the first out, but walked Lonnie Smith.

That brought up Terry Pendleton, who had hit a homer in the fifth. This time, Pendleton tapped a slow roller between the pitcher's mound and first base. Nobody could get to it and Pendleton had an infield single. Now the bases were loaded with one out.

The Braves donned their rally caps to urge on Ron Gant. The Twins brought in Carl Willis to pitch to him.

If Gant could get the bat on the ball and stay out of a double play, he would almost certainly drive in the tying run. A hit would put the Braves in the lead.

Gant hit a grounder to short, not too hard. Mark Lemke bolted for the plate. The Twins could have tried to nail him at home, but went for the inning-ending double play instead. They got the first out, but Ron Gant streaked across the first-base bag just ahead of the throw. As the umpire made the safe sign, Gant pumped his fist triumphantly. Mark Lemke scored and the game was tied at 3–3.

It seemed like every time one team got a lead in this World Series, the other would come back and tie the game. It wasn't that the losing team scored fewer runs;

they just ran out of innings. Now the innings were dwindling to a precious few in Game 6, and everybody knew that the next run could be the winning run.

The Twins got Kirby Puckett to second base in the eighth inning but couldn't bring him around. Terry Pendleton banged out four hits for the Braves but only scored when he hit his homer in the fifth inning.

Tension mounted as the game remained deadlocked through the eighth and ninth innings. It was going to be another nail-biting extra-innings game. One swing of a Twins bat and Minnesota would win the game and tie the Series. One swing of an Atlanta bat and the World Series could be over.

Both Steve Avery and Scott Erickson were long gone. The relief pitchers for both teams were doing their jobs. Neither team could push across a run in the tenth inning.

Kirby Puckett led off the bottom of the eleventh for the Twins. Puckett had fought his way out of the slums of Chicago's South Side to become one of the most respected, popular, and wealthiest athletes in the world. Through the first five games of the Series, he was hitting .167 and had more strikeouts than hits. But in Game 6 he had already singled, tripled, stolen a base, scored a run, driven in a run on a sacrifice fly, and made an impossible catch in which he leaped four feet against the centerfield wall. Another worst to first.

"Kirby! Kirby!" screamed the home crowd. They wanted to squeeze one more bit of heroics from Puckett.

Atlanta manager Bobby Cox brought in Charlie Leibrandt to pitch. Leibrandt had struck out Puckett twice in Game 1. Both times, he had used his change-up. Puckett remembered. He told himself to watch for the change-up and try to hit one high in the strike zone.

Strike one, called. Ball one. Ball two, low. The count was 2–1, and Leibrandt had yet to throw a change-up.

On the next pitch, he did. Puckett got what he was looking for and unloaded on it. The ball jumped off his bat.

In centerfield, Ron Gant looked up. For a moment he thought he had a play, but the ball sailed far over his head and into the seats.

Home run! Game over! Twins 4, Braves 3. Bedlam in the Metrodome! Puckett pumped his fists as he motored around the bases. There was a mob scene to greet him at home plate.

Charlie Leibrandt walked off the mound with his face buried in his right arm.

Puckett's blast brought back memories of Carlton Fisk in the 1975 World Series. It was a similar situation— Game 6 had been tied in extra innings, and a leadoff homer won the game to tie the World Series.

"I don't care about making history," said Puckett. "I just want to play tomorrow."

Thanks to his homer, he would play Game 7 tomorrow. The Twins had come back from the brink.

"Whatever happens tomorrow, it's been a great Series,"

Kirby Puckett told reporters after the game. "This is like being in a 15-round fight. I'm so drained, I don't know what to do."

Minnesota pitching coach Terry Crowley was walking around in circles in the clubhouse, muttering, "It's unbelievable. Unbelievable."

Ten minutes after Kirby Puckett touched home plate to win the game, the fans were still on their feet, cheering. They didn't want to go home.

GAME 7.   How can Game 7 of the 1991 World Series be described in mere words? Simply put, it was one of the most exciting baseball games ever played.

It was a foggy night in Minneapolis, but nobody noticed inside the Metrodome, where the air crackled with tension even before the game began. The season had come down to one final game. Everybody was ready to play. Starting pitchers were ready to relieve, pinch run, or pinch hit if necessary. There would be no tomorrow.

It was 24-year-old John Smoltz pitching against his boyhood idol, Jack Morris. Smoltz had finished the season with eight straight wins, plus two more in the National League playoff. Morris had won the first game of the season, the All-Star Game, the first game of the American League playoff, and the first game of the World Series. Each pitcher wore determination on his face before the game. This was no time to be loose.

When he stepped into the batter's box to start the game, Lonnie Smith turned to Twins catcher Brian Harper and stuck out his hand. Harper shook it. It was a silent recognition that the war was almost over, and each side had fought gallantly.

Smoltz and Morris methodically retired the side in order in the first inning. Both teams got singles in the second, but neither came close to staging a rally. Smoltz and Morris were too strong.

Zeroes started piling up on the scoreboard. Despite getting several hits, neither team scored in the third, fourth, or fifth innings.

Some fans like high-scoring games, with lots of homers and extra base hits. A pitcher's duel can be boring. But not a pitcher's duel in the seventh game of the World Series. When somebody gets a double in a 9–3 game in April, it doesn't mean much. But with the whole season on the line, and the score 0–0 in the late innings, a double is a huge event.

In five innings of this game, an Atlanta runner reached second or third base. For the Twins, runners were in scoring position in four innings. But not a single runner had reached the one base that counted—home plate.

The two warriors, Morris and Smoltz, buzzed through the hitters in the sixth and seventh innings. Morris in particular seemed to be getting stronger as the game went on, using his fastball, splitter, and occasional change-up effectively. The way these two were pitching, fans had the feeling that whichever team could manage to score a run was going to win it.

Nobody was getting up to buy popcorn. Fans only went to the bathroom if it was an emergency.

The eighth inning of this game ranks up there with some of the most exciting in history. Lonnie Smith led off for Atlanta. Despite his three homers earlier in the Series, Smith was hitting just .182. Morris fooled him with a pitch, but Lonnie checked his swing and blooped a soft single into rightfield.

Morris got two strikes on Terry Pendleton, but the National League's leading hitter then slammed an outside fastball to the gap in left centerfield.

Lonnie Smith should have been able to score on the hit. He had stolen 68 bases in 1982, and was still one of the fastest runners in the game.

But Lonnie got faked out of his boots by a rookie. When the ball was hit, Twins second baseman Chuck Knoblauch pretended it was a ground ball. He pantomimed fielding the grounder and tossing it to shortstop Greg Gagne near second base.

Lonnie Smith lost sight of Pendleton's shot, which had bounced off the wall. He didn't look at his third-base coach, Jimy Williams. When he saw Knoblauch and Gagne doing what they would be doing if Pendleton had hit a grounder, he stopped running.

Finally, Lonnie realized he'd been duped. He started running again, but he could only make it to third base. If

Lonnie hadn't stopped, he would have scored the first run of the game easily. And if Smith couldn't score and the Braves lost the game, his baserunning blunder would go down in history.

But Braves had runners on second and third with nobody out. Just about anything would drive Smith home.

The Minnesota infield moved in. At this stage of the game, they had to keep that run from scoring. Ron Gant, who had hit 32 homers each of the last two seasons, was up. No homer this time. Gant bounced out weakly to first. Kent Hrbek scooped the ball up quickly and tagged him. One out. The runners were forced to stay at second and third.

David Justice was up, with Sid Bream to follow. Twins manager Tom Kelly went out to the mound for a chat with Jack Morris.

"Keep him in!" chanted the crowd. *"Keep him in!"*

"What do you think?" asked Kelly.

"I think I can get Bream out," Morris replied.

Kelly told Morris to walk Justice intentionally to load the bases and set up a possible double play.

It was Sid Bream's chance to be the hero. He took ball one, then fouled off the next two pitches. It was obvious that he was trying to hit the ball in the air so Lonnie Smith could tag up from third. With two strikes, Bream had to protect the plate.

He hit the next pitch sharply on the ground to first. All three runners took off. Twins first baseman Kent Hrbek grabbed the bouncing ball cleanly and threw it home. Catcher Brian Harper caught it, stepped on the plate to force out Lonnie Smith, and whipped the ball back to Hrbek at first.

Out! Double play. Hrbek pumped his fist after he caught the ball. Jack Morris had fought his way out of a desperate situation. The game remained scoreless.

The bottom of the eighth was just as wild. Twins pinch hitter Randy Bush went for Smoltz's first pitch of the inning and singled. Al Newman was sent in to pinch run. Dan Gladden tried to bunt Newman to second, but fouled two pitches off. With the bunt sign taken off, Gladden flied out. One out.

Chuck Knoblauch was up, and the hit-and-run play was on. Newman was running with the pitch and Knoblauch lined a single to right. Now there were Twins runners at first and third with one out and last night's hero—Kirby Puckett—coming up.

John Smoltz had put on a tremendous performance, but Atlanta manager Bobby Cox decided he'd had enough. Mike Stanton came in with instructions to walk Puckett intentionally. That loaded the bases for a possible double play. It also allowed Atlanta to pitch to Kent Hrbek, who hadn't had a hit in his last 15 at-bats. Hrbek, however, did hit a grand slam home run in the 1987 World Series.

Ball one. Foul ball, strike one. Ball two.

On the next pitch, Hrbek hit a liner toward second.

Mark Lemke darted to his right. He speared the ball for the second out, and his momentum carried him across the second-base bag. Unassisted double play to end the inning!

Incredible. Each team had loaded the bases with less than two outs. Each team had pulled off a double play to preserve the scoreless tie.

Now it was the ninth inning, and there was a lot of nail biting going on in the dugouts, in the stands, and in the living rooms of America. The only person who seemed calm was Jack Morris. He retired the Braves 1–2–3. The man was a machine.

When the Twins came up in the bottom of the ninth, their mission was clear. Score a run, now, any way possible, and win the World Series.

Chili Davis fouled off five pitches from Mike Stanton and then hit a long single to right centerfield. The winning run was on. Stanton got two strikes on Brian Harper, who then surprised everybody by squaring around to bunt. Harper dropped the ball expertly between the pitcher's mound and first base. Nobody could touch it. Now the Twins had runners at first and second with nobody out. A base hit would win the World Series.

Mike Stanton strained his knee chasing the bunt and had to leave the game. Alejandro Pena came in to pitch for the Braves. Shane Mack was up. Pena kept the ball low, and Mack slapped a grounder to second. Lemke gloved it, flipped to Belliard, whose throw to Bream was right there. Another double play!

The Braves got those two important outs, but Chili Davis was at third. The World Series winning run was 90 feet away.

Mike Pagliarulo was up, and the Braves decided to walk him intentionally and pitch to Al Newman (.191) instead. Newman had come in as a pinch runner the inning before.

Two could play at that game. The Twins sent up Paul Sorrento (.255) to pinch hit for Newman.

Strike one. Strike two. Foul ball. Foul ball. 0–2 count.

Strike three! Inning over! What a performance by Alejandro Pena!

At the end of nine innings, the scoreboard looked like this:

Braves 000 000 000

Twins 000 000 000

It was like two people having a staring contest, each trying desperately not to blink.

The last time the seventh game of a World Series went into extra innings was way back in 1924 (see Chapter Two). The winning team that year was the Washington Senators—who moved to Minnesota in 1961 and became the Twins.

Lonnie Smith's baserunning blunder in the eighth was looming larger. If he hadn't stopped to look at the scenery, he would have scored and the Braves would be in the clubhouse squirting champagne all over each other. Instead, this became the first World Series in history to have the seventh game go scoreless through nine innings.

Before the tenth inning, Minnesota manager Tom Kelly pulled Jack Morris aside.

"That's enough, Jack," said Kelly.

"I'm fine," Morris replied. "If I wasn't fine, I'd tell you."

"Jack, you've done your part. It's time for the boys to carry some of the load."

"I've still got my stuff. I want to stay."

Kelly consented to let Morris stay in the game. Morris was right. He *did* still have his stuff. Morris retired the Braves 1–2–3 in the tenth. He had thrown 125 pitches in the game.

By this time, it was almost midnight on the East Coast. Adults were worrying about getting up to go to work the next morning. Kids were begging to stay up to watch *one* more inning. Nobody wanted to go to bed and miss the finish.

Alejandro Pena was still on the mound for the Braves in the bottom of the tenth. The top of the order was up for the Twins. Pena jammed Dan Gladden and broke his bat, but Gladden muscled the ball over the infield and into leftfield.

The ball bounced high off the artificial turf. Gladden never slowed down. He decided to stretch the single into a double and slid into second just ahead of the tag. Because of Gladden's hustle, the Twins had the winning run in scoring position with nobody out.

It was a bunting situation, and Chuck Knoblauch

tapped the ball down the third-base line perfectly. Dan Gladden was at third base now with one out.

A fly ball now would win it all. The Atlanta outfield moved in.

Two long-ball threats, Kirby Puckett and Kent Hrbek, were coming up. Atlanta had no choice but to walk both of them intentionally. That loaded the bases. Pena would have to pitch to somebody.

That somebody was scheduled to be Jarvis Brown, a utility man who had come in as a pinch runner in the ninth inning. With 37 major league at-bats, he wasn't the right man to bring in with the bases loaded in the bottom of the tenth in the seventh game of the World Series.

It was exactly midnight, East Coast time.

In the stands, Kathleen Larkin saw her husband Gene step out of the Minnesota dugout and begin swinging a bat in the on-deck circle. She hid her eyes. She couldn't bear to watch.

As a schoolboy, Gene Larkin had attended Columbia University and he broke all of Lou Gehrig's records there. He hadn't had as much success as Gehrig during his five years in the majors, but he was a consistent hitter. From 1987 to 1990, he hit .266, .267, .267, and .269. In 1991 he hit .286 with two homers.

Larkin was looking for a pitch in the strike zone. He had to get the ball to the outfield so Gladden could tag up from third and score. His left knee was injured. He could hit, but he could barely run. If he hit a ground ball here, it would be an almost automatic inning-ending double play. And the Braves had pulled off double plays to get out of jams in the sixth, eighth, and ninth innings.

The Atlanta outfield moved just 30 yards behind the infield. Larkin was a switch hitter, so he batted left-handed against the right-handed Alejandro Pena.

Pena's first pitch was high and outside. It wasn't the best pitch to hit, but it was a good pitch to lift a fly ball to the outfield.

Larkin hit it.

Almost instantly, Gene Larkin raised his fist in the air. He was the first person in America to know the World Series was over. As his bat made contact with the ball, he could feel that he'd hit the ball in the air, and that he'd hit it solidly.

The ball soared toward left centerfield. Atlanta leftfielder Brian Hunter could have backpedaled and caught it, but it wouldn't have made any difference. Gladden would have tagged up and scored no matter what. Hunter let the ball sail over his head.

The Minnesota Twins had won the game by the score of 1–0, and they'd won what many would say was the greatest World Series ever played.

Fans had swarmed onto the field and streaked past the third-base line even before Dan Gladden happily scampered home to score the winning run. The Twins leaped and danced out of their dugout to congratulate Gladden for scoring the winning run and Larkin for knocking it in.

"Where's my wife?" shouted Gene Larkin as he pushed his way past well-wishers. "Where's my wife?"

After it was all over, players on both teams agreed they had participated in a classic. Terry Pendleton of the Braves told a reporter, "People who saw these games aged ten or twenty years." His teammate Mark Lemke said, "The only thing better would have been if we stopped after nine innings and cut the trophy in half."

Perhaps Kent Hrbek summed it up best. "This is a good lesson for life," he said. "It shows anyone that no matter how down you are, you always have a chance to come back."

When it was all over, pitcher John Smoltz sat alone with his thoughts in the Atlanta dugout. His side had lost the final battle, but it had been a thrilling war. (AP/Wide World Photos)

In the Atlanta clubhouse, David Justice walked over to Mark Lemke. He told Lemke that Chili Davis of the Twins wanted to see him in the laundry room that connected the two clubhouses.

It sounded like trouble. But Lemke was not one to shy away from confrontation. He went into the laundry room. Several Twins were there.

"You killed us, Lemmer," said Davis, who threw his arms around Lemke and gave him a hug.

"Man, that was fun," Lemke told the Twins. "Let's do it again next year."

For Baseball Trivia Lovers . . .

♦ Mark Lemke *did* do it again next year. The Atlanta Braves won the pennant again in 1992. Again they lost the World Series, this time to the Toronto Blue Jays. In 1993, Atlanta won their division again, but lost the play-offs to the Philadelphia Phillies.

♦ The ace of the Toronto pitching staff that year was none other than Jack Morris. Morris went to the Blue Jays as a free agent after the 1991 World Series. As a 37-year-old, he had his winningest season ever: 21–6.

♦ Back to 1991. Rick Aguilera, who was the winning pitcher of Game 6, was also the winning pitcher of Game 6 in the 1986 World Series.

♦ This was the first time any team went from last place to first place in a single season. But back in the days when there were more than six teams in each division, a few teams came from even farther back to win a pennant. These teams came from sixth place to first in a single season: the 1907 Tigers, 1915 Phillies, 1933 Giants, 1944 Browns, 1961 Reds, 1965 Dodgers and Twins, and the 1967 Cardinals. These teams came from seventh to first: the 1926 Yankees, 1946 Red Sox, and 1959 Dodgers. Finally, the 1967 Red Sox and 1969 Mets went all the way from ninth place to first.

♦ The Minnesota Twins are the only team to win a World Series without winning a single game in the opposing team's ballpark. They've done it twice, in 1987 and 1991.

♦ David Justice was born on April 14, 1966, two days after the Atlanta Braves played their first game.

♦ Minnesota backup catcher Junior Ortiz had a thing with names and numbers. His real name was Adalberto, but during a slump early in the season he changed it to Joe. Ortiz named his son "Junior," so the boy's full name is Junior Ortiz Junior. Ortiz was one of the few players in baseball who chose to wear the number zero on his uniform.

BOX SCORES

Game 1

```
Atlanta        000.001 010—2 6 1
Minnesota      001.031 00x—5 9 1
```

Atlanta	AB	R	H	BI	BB	SO	Avg.
Smith dh	3	1	0	0	1	0	.000
Treadway 2b	3	1	1	0	1	2	.333
Pendleton 3b	4	0	0	0	0	0	.000
Justice rf	2	0	1	0	2	0	.500
Gant cf	4	0	3	2	0	0	.750
Bream 1b	4	0	0	0	0	1	.000
Hunter lf	4	0	0	0	0	1	.000
Olson c	3	0	1	0	1	0	.333
Belliard ss	1	0	0	0	0	0	.000
b-Blauser ph-ss	2	0	0	0	0	0	.000
Totals	30	2	6	2	5	3	

Minnesota	AB	R	H	BI	BB	SO	Avg.
Gladden lf	2	1	0	0	2	0	.000
Knoblauch 2b	3	0	3	1	1	0	1.000
Puckett cf	4	0	0	0	0	2	.000
Davis dh	3	0	0	0	1	1	.000
Harper c	4	0	2	0	0	0	.500
Mack rf	4	0	0	0	0	1	.000
Hrbek 1b	4	2	2	1	0	1	.500
Leius 3b	2	1	1	0	0	0	.500
a-Pagliarulo ph-3b	1	0	0	0	0	0	.000
Gagne ss	3	1	1	3	0	1	.333
Totals	30	5	9	5	4	6	

Atlanta	IP	H	R	ER	BB	SO	NP	ERA
Leibrandt L, 0-1	4	7	4	4	1	3	79	9.00
Clancy	2	1	1	1	2	0	32	4.50
Wohlers	1	1	0	0	1	1	18	0.00
Stanton	1	0	0	0	0	2	11	0.00

Minnesota	IP	H	R	ER	BB	SO	NP	ERA
Morris W, 1-0	7	5	2	2	4	3	100	2.57
Guthrie	⅔	0	0	0	1	0	7	0.00
Aguilera S, 1	1⅓	1	0	0	0	0	18	0.00

Game 2

Atlanta	AB	R	H	BI	BB	SO	Avg.
LoSmith dh	3	0	0	0	0	0	.000
Pendleton 3b	4	0	2	0	0	1	.250
Gant cf	4	0	1	0	0	0	.500
Justice rf	4	1	1	0	0	1	.333
Bream 1b	4	0	1	0	0	1	.125
Hunter lf	3	0	1	0	1	0	.143
Olson c	4	1	1	0	0	1	.286
Lemke 2b	3	0	0	0	0	1	.000
a-Gregg ph	1	0	0	0	0	0	.000
Belliard ss	2	0	1	1	0	0	.333
Totals	32	2	8	2	0	6	

Minnesota	AB	R	H	BI	BB	SO	Avg.
Gladden lf	4	0	0	0	0	1	.000
Knoblauch 2b	3	1	0	0	1	0	.500
Puckett cf	4	0	0	0	0	1	.000
CDavis dh	3	1	1	2	0	0	.167
Harper c	2	0	1	0	1	0	.500
Mack rf	3	0	0	0	0	2	.000
Hrbek 1b	2	0	0	1	1	1	.333
Leius 3b	3	1	1	0	0	0	.400
Gagne ss	3	0	1	0	0	1	.333
Totals	27	3	4	3	3	6	

```
Atlanta        010 010 000—2  8 1
Minnesota      200 000 01x—3  4 1
```

a-struck out for Lemke in the 9th. E—Justice (1), Leius (1). LOB—Atlanta 6, Minnesota 3. 2B—Bream (1), Olson (1). HR—CDavis (1) off Glavine, Leius (1) off Glavine. RBI—Hunter (1), Belliard (1), CDavis 2 (2), Leius (1). S—LoSmith. SF—Hunter, Belliard. GIDP—Puckett, Leius. Runners left in scoring position—Atlanta 2 (Justice, Lemke); Minnesota 1 (Puckett). Runners moved up—Lemke, Knoblauch. DP—Atlanta 2 (Pendleton and Bream), (Glavine, Lemke and Bream).

Atlanta	IP	H	R	ER	BB	SO	NP	ERA
Glavine L, 0-1	8	4	3	3	3	6	108	3.38

Minnesota	IP	H	R	ER	BB	SO	NP	ERA
Tapani W, 1-0	8	7	2	2	0	3	105	2.25
Aguilera S, 2	1	1	0	0	0	3	19	0.00

Game 3

Minnesota	AB	R	H	BI	BB	SO	Avg.
Gladden lf	6	1	3	0	0	1	.250
Knoblauch 2b	5	0	1	1	0	0	.364
Hrbek 1b	6	0	1	0	0	2	.250
Puckett cf	4	1	1	1	2	2	.083
Mack rf	4	0	0	0	0	2	.000
Willis p	0	0	0	0	0	0	—
g-Sorrento ph	1	0	0	0	0	1	.000
Guthrie p	0	0	0	0	0	0	—
i-Aguilera ph-p	1	0	0	0	0	0	.000
Leius 3b	3	0	0	0	0	1	.250
d-Pagliarulo ph-3b	1	0	0	0	1	0	.000
j-Newman ph-3b	1	0	0	0	0	0	.000
Gagne ss	5	0	0	0	0	1	.182
Ortiz c	2	0	1	0	0	0	.500
b-Harper ph-c	3	1	1	0	0	0	.444
Erickson p	1	0	0	0	0	1	.000
West p	0	0	0	0	0	0	—
Leach p	0	0	0	0	0	0	—
a-Larkin ph	1	0	1	0	0	0	1.000
Bedrosian p	0	0	0	0	0	0	—
c-CDavis ph	1	1	1	2	0	0	.286
JBrown rf	0	0	0	0	0	0	—
e-Bush ph-rf	2	0	0	0	0	0	.000
Totals	47	4	10	4	2	13	

Atlanta	AB	R	H	BI	BB	SO	Avg.
LoSmith lf	4	1	1	1	0	1	.100
KMitchell lf	2	0	0	0	0	1	.000
Pendleton 3b	4	1	0	0	2	0	.167
Gant cf	6	0	0	0	0	2	.286
Justice rf	6	2	2	1	0	1	.333
Bream 1b	3	0	1	0	1	0	.182
h-Hunter ph-1b	2	0	0	0	0	0	.111
Olson c	3	1	1	1	3	0	.300
Lemke 2b	5	0	2	1	1	1	.250
Belliard ss	3	0	1	1	1	0	.333
i-Blauser ph-ss	1	0	0	0	0	0	.000
Avery p	3	0	0	0	0	2	.000
Pena p	0	0	0	0	0	0	—
f-Treadway ph	0	0	0	0	0	0	.333
Stanton p	0	0	0	0	0	0	—
k-Cabrera ph	1	0	0	0	0	0	.000
Wohlers p	0	0	0	0	0	0	—
Mercker p	0	0	0	0	0	0	—
Clancy p	0	0	0	0	0	0	—
Totals	43	5	8	5	8	6	

```
Minnesota      100 000 120 000—4  10 1
Atlanta        010 120 000 001—5   8 2
```

Minnesota	IP	H	R	ER	BB	SO	NP	ERA
Erickson	4⅔	5	4	3	2	3	88	5.79
West	0	0	0	0	2	0	10	—
Leach	⅓	0	0	0	0	1	4	0.00
Bedrosian	2	0	0	0	1	2	25	0.00
Willis	2	0	0	0	2	0	23	0.00
Guthrie	2	1	0	0	1	1	37	0.00
Aguilera L, 0-1	⅔	2	1	1	0	1	17	3.00

Atlanta	IP	H	R	ER	BB	SO	NP	ERA
Avery	7	4	3	2	0	5	84	2.57
Pena	2	4	1	1	0	4	41	4.50
Stanton	2	1	0	0	1	3	18	0.00
Wohlers	⅓	1	0	0	0	0	8	0.00
Mercker	⅓	0	0	0	1	4	0.00
Clancy W, 1-0	⅓	0	0	0	1	0	3	3.86

BOX SCORES

Game 4

Minnesota	AB	R	H	BI	BB	SO	Avg.
Gladden lf	4	0	0	0	0	0	.188
Knoblauch 2b	3	0	1	0	1	1	.357
Puckett cf	4	0	1	0	0	0	.125
Hrbek 1b	4	0	0	0	0	1	.188
Harper c	4	1	2	0	0	0	.462
Mack rf	4	0	0	0	0	2	.000
Pagliarulo 3b	3	1	3	2	0	0	.600
e-Leius ph	1	0	0	0	0	0	.222
Bedrosian p	0	0	0	0	0	0	—
Gagne ss	3	0	0	0	0	3	.143
Morris p	2	0	0	0	0	1	.000
a-Larkin ph	1	0	0	0	0	0	.500
Willis p	0	0	0	0	0	0	—
Guthrie p	0	0	0	0	0	0	—
Newman 3b	0	0	0	0	0	0	.000
Totals	33	2	7	2	1	8	

Atlanta	AB	R	H	BI	BB	SO	Avg.
LoSmith lf	4	1	2	1	0	1	.214
Pendleton 3b	4	1	2	1	0	0	.250
Gant cf	3	0	1	0	1	0	.294
Justice rf	3	0	0	0	1	1	.267
Bream 1b	3	0	0	0	0	1	.143
d-Hunter ph-1b	1	0	0	0	0	0	.100
Olson c	3	0	0	1	1	1	.231
Lemke 2b	4	1	3	0	0	0	.417
Belliard ss	2	0	0	0	0	0	.250
b-Treadway ph	1	0	0	0	0	0	.250
Blauser ss	0	0	0	1	0	0	.000
Smoltz p	2	0	0	0	0	1	.000
c-Gregg ph	1	0	0	0	1	0	.000
Wohlers p	0	0	0	0	0	0	—
Stanton p	0	0	0	0	0	0	—
f-Cabrera ph	0	0	0	0	0	0	.000
g-Willard ph	0	0	1	0	0	0	.000
Totals	31	3	8	3	4	6	

Minnesota							
	010	000	100	—2	7	0	

Atlanta							
	001	000	101	—3	8	0	

Minnesota	IP	H	R	ER	BB	SO	NP	ERA
Morris	6	6	1	1	3	4	94	2.08
Willis	1⅓	1	1	1	0	1	17	2.70
Guthrie L, 0-1	1	1	1	1	1	1	14	2.45
Bedrosian	½	0	0	0	0	0	4	0.00

Atlanta	IP	H	R	ER	BB	SO	NP	ERA
Smoltz	7	7	2	0	7	0	96	2.57
Wohlers	½	0	0	0	1	0	10	0.00
Stanton W, 1-0	1⅓	0	0	0	1	0	26	0.00

Game 5

MINNESOTA	ab	r	h	bi		ATLANTA	ab	r	h	bi
Gladden lf	5	1	1	0		LoSmith lf	5	1	1	1
Knblch 2b	3	1	1	0		KtMchl lf	0	0	0	0
Bdrsian p	0	0	0	0		Pndltn 3b	4	3	2	0
Ortiz c	1	0	0	1		Gant cf	4	3	3	1
Puckett cf	2	1	1	0		Justice rf	5	2	2	5
JBrown cf	2	0	0	0		Bream 1b	2	0	0	0
CDavis rf	3	2	1	0		Hunter 1b	2	2	2	2
Wllis p	0	0	0	0		Olson c	5	1	3	0
Harper c	2	0	0	1		StClre p	0	0	0	0
Bush rf	1	0	0	0		Lemke 2b	4	2	2	3
Leius 3b	2	0	1	1		Blhard ss	4	0	2	2
West p	0	0	0	0		Glavine p	2	0	0	0
Newman 2b	1	0	1	1		Mrcker p	0	0	0	0
Hrbek 1b	3	0	0	1		Gregg ph	0	0	0	0
Srrento 1b	0	0	0	0		Clancy p	1	0	0	0
Gagne ss	4	0	1	0		Cbrera c	0	0	0	0
Tapani p	1	0	0	0						
Larkin ph	1	0	0	0						
Leach p	0	0	0	0						
Pgirulo 3b	2	0	0	0						
Totals	33	5	7	5		Totals	39	14	17	14

Minnesota							
	000	003	011	—5			

Atlanta							
	000	410	63x	—14			

E—Harper (1), Pendleton (2). DP—Minnesota 1. LOB—Minnesota 7, Atlanta 5. 2B—Gagne (1), Pendleton (2), Belliard (1). 3B—Gladden (2), Newman (1), Gant (1), Lemke 2 (3). HR—LoSmith (3), Justice (2), Hunter (1). SB—Justice (2), Olson (1). CS—Leius (1) S—Puckett.

Minnesota	IP	H	R	ER	BB	SO
Tapani L,1-1	4	6	4	4	2	4
Leach	2	2	1	1	0	1
West	0	2	4	4	2	0
Bedrosian	1	3	2	2	0	1
Willis	1	4	3	3	0	0

Atlanta	IP	H	R	ER	BB	SO
Glavine W,1-1	5 1-3	4	3	3	4	2
Mercker	2-3	0	0	0	0	2
Clancy	2	1	1	1	1	2
StClare	1	1	1	1	0	0

Game 6

ATLANTA	ab	r	h	bi		MINNESOTA	ab	r	h	bi
LoSmith dh	3	1	0	0		Gldden lf	4	1	0	0
Pndltn 3b	5	1	4	2		Knblch 2b	5	1	1	0
Gant cf	5	0	0	1		Puckett cf	4	2	3	3
Justice rf	4	0	0	0		CDavis dh	4	0	0	0
Bream 1b	4	0	1	0		Mack rf	4	0	2	1
KtMchl lf	0	0	0	0		Leius 3b	3	0	2	0
Hunter lf	5	0	0	0		Pgirulo 3b	1	0	0	0
Olson c	5	0	0	0		Hrbek 1b	4	0	0	0
Lemke 2b	4	1	2	0		Ortiz c	2	0	0	0
Gregg ph	0	0	0	0		Harper c	2	0	0	0
Bliard ss	2	0	1	0		Gagne ss	4	0	1	0
Blauser ss	2	0	1	0						
Totals	39	3	9	3		Totals	37	4	9	4

Atlanta							
	000	020	100	00—3			

Minnesota							
	200	010	000	01—4			

No outs when winning run scored.

E—Hunter (1). DP—Atlanta 2, Minnesota 2. LOB—Atlanta 7, Minnesota 5. 2B—Mack (1). 3B—Puckett (1). HR—Pendleton (2), Puckett (2). SB—Gladden (2), Puckett (1). CS—KtMitchell (1). SF—Puckett.

Atlanta	IP	H	R	ER	BB	SO
Avery	6	6	3	3	1	3
Stanton	2	2	0	0	0	1
Pena	2	0	0	0	0	2
Leibrandt L,0-2	0	1	1	1	0	0

Minnesota	IP	H	R	ER	BB	SO
Erickson	6	5	3	3	2	2
Guthrie	1-3	1	0	0	1	1
Willis	2 2-3	1	0	0	0	1
Aguilera W,1-1	2	2	0	0	0	0

Game 7

Atlanta							
	000	000	000	0—0	7	0	
Minnesota	000	000	000	1—1	10	0	

Atlanta	AB	R	H	BI	BB	SO	Avg.
Smith dh	4	0	2	0	1	1	.231
Pendleton 3b	5	0	1	0	0	0	.367
Gant cf	4	0	0	0	0	2	.267
Justice rf	3	0	1	0	1	1	.259
Bream 1b	4	0	0	0	0	1	.125
Hunter lf	4	0	1	0	0	1	.190
Olson c	4	0	0	0	0	1	.222
Lemke 2b	4	0	1	0	0	0	.417
Belliard ss	2	0	1	0	0	1	.375
c-Blauser ph-ss	1	0	0	0	0	0	.167
Totals	35	0	7	0	2	8	

Minnesota	AB	R	H	BI	BB	SO	Avg.
Gladden lf	5	1	3	0	0	1	.233
Knoblauch 2b	4	0	1	0	0	0	.308
Puckett cf	2	0	0	3	1	0	.250
Hrbek 1b	3	0	0	1	0	1	.115
Davis dh	4	0	1	0	0	1	.222
2-Brown pr-ph	0	0	0	0	0	0	.000
d-Larkin ph	1	0	1	0	0	0	.500
Harper c	4	0	2	0	0	0	.381
Mack rf	4	0	1	0	0	2	.130
Pagliarulo 3b	3	0	0	0	1	0	.273
Gagne ss	2	0	0	0	0	0	.167
a-Bush ph	1	0	1	0	0	0	.250
1-Newman pr-ss	0	0	0	0	0	0	.500
b-Sorrento ph	1	0	0	0	1	0	.000
Leius ss	0	0	0	0	0	0	.357
Totals	34	1	10	1	5	5	

About This Book

After the 1991 World Series was over, many experts proclaimed it to be the most exciting Series ever. That gave me the idea to find out which *other* World Series were the most exciting, and describe them in a book.

I had one big problem when I set out to write it—I wasn't *born* until 1955 (two weeks after the Brooklyn Dodgers won their only World Series). Through no fault of my own, I had already missed three of the most exciting World Series. But I would still have to describe them, and in detail.

There are no audio or video tapes of the 1912 Series that I could use for research. Television was only a science fiction fantasy in 1912, and the first baseball game to be broadcast by radio wouldn't be played for another nine years (August 5, 1921, between the Pirates and the Phillies).

In 1912, people learned of events almost entirely through newspapers. Articles about the World Series were filled with wonderful details—the colors of the uniforms, what the fans shouted, which celebrities were in the crowd, and so on. Reading these old newspapers enabled me to recreate the feeling of the games.

Radio had arrived in time for the 1924 World Series. But

the tape recorder wasn't invented for another five years, so those games are lost to history. Once again I relied on newspapers for the play-by-play. Most of the information in the first two chapters of this book come from *The New York Times* reports the day after each game.

I didn't make up a single fact, quote, or passage that appears in this book. Everything has been documented— in a newspaper story, magazine article, book, or tape.

For example, toward the end of Chapter 1, Fred Snodgrass of the New York Giants hovered under a fly ball and dropped it—one of the most famous errors in baseball history. When I said Snodgrass shouted, "I got it!" I didn't just write that because outfielders frequently shout "I got it." Here is the description of that play as it appeared in *The New York Times* the next day:

Is Mathewson, apprehensive as he walks to the box? He is not. All the confidence that was his when the blood of youth ran strong in his supple muscles is his now. Even though the mountainous Engle faces him—the same Engle who brought in the two runs of the Red Sox on Monday—he shows not a quiver, and he is right. All that Engle can do with the elusive drop served up is to hoist it high between centre and right fields. Snodgrass and Murray are both within reach of it, with time to spare. Snodgrass yells, "I got it," and sets himself to take it with ease, as he has taken hundreds of the sort. . . .

I love the way sportswriters wrote back then. This is how the *Times* described Smokey Joe Wood of the Red Sox: *"His face paled and his jaws were set tightly as he faced the frenzied multitude which howled for his downfall."*

I had fun going to the library and digging through old issues of the *Times* on microfilm. For a dime or so, the machines make a copy of any page. That's how I collected the headlines on the first page of each chapter.

Many American families got their first TV set just to watch the 1947 World Series, and it turned out to be a great one. Highlights of that Series can be seen in baseball history tapes you can rent in most video stores. I supplemented these with newspapers, magazine articles, and books such as Roger Kahn's *The Boys of Summer*.

By 1975, I could experience the World Series as it was happening, and I remember watching that one on television. But that was nearly 20 years ago, and I had to refresh my memories. In addition to newspapers, *Sports Illustrated* was helpful. So was Peter Golenbock's book *Fenway*.

By 1991, I had written several baseball books and decided it might be a good idea to throw tapes in my VCR and record the World Series as I watched it—just in case I might need it someday. Coincidentally, it turned out to be one of the best Series ever. I didn't have to go far to research that chapter—I just popped in my tapes and watched the Series all over again.

You may be wondering who decided these five Series were the most exciting ever played. Well, *I* did.

Here's how I did it: First I looked up all the World Series that lasted seven games, because that means the teams were evenly matched and the Series came down to one final confrontation.

Second, I looked for Series in which the scores of the games were close. Tight games are tense games. Many people think of the 1960 World Series as one of the most exciting because it ended with Bill Mazeroski's dramatic home run. But three of the games were boring blowouts (16–3, 10–0, 12–0). I couldn't count that as one of the greatest World Series ever played. The 1991 Series, on the other hand, featured five one-run games, and three of them ended in extra innings.

Eventually, I was able to narrow the list down to the five World Series described in this book.

So that's how I found all the information that appears in *World Series Classics*. In researching this book, I learned a lot about baseball that I hadn't known. I hope you learned a lot by reading it, too.

—Dan Gutman

Index

ABOUT THE AUTHOR

Dan Gutman is the author of *Baseball's Biggest Bloopers*, *Baseball's Greatest Games*, *Baseball Babylon*, and other sports books for young readers.